THE
ONEWORLD
BOOK OF
PRAYER

THE
ONEWORLD
BOOK OF
PRAYER

A Treasury of Prayers from Around the World

COMPILED BY JULIET MABEY

ONEWORLD

OXFORD

THE ONEWORLD BOOK OF PRAYER

Oneworld Publications
(Sales and Editorial)
185 Banbury Road
Oxford OX2 7AR
England
http://www.oneworld-publications.com

Oneworld Publications
(US Marketing Office)
160 N Washington St.
4th floor, Boston
MA 02114

ISBN 1–85168–203–1

Cover and text design by Design Deluxe, Bath
Printed by Graphicom Srl, Vicenza, Italy

CONTENTS

P R E F A C E

GATHERED TOGETHER here are prayers from all over the world and down the ages, from East and West, and drawn both from the oral traditions of primitive religions and the sacred texts of world faiths. Together they show us that, at their most essential, prayers are the same all over the world, in every religion and every century.

Whether one is a Christian in the Middle East, a Muslim in Paris, or a Native American, lifting one's heart to the divine in the depths of sorrow or at the height of joy is a universal human act. Prayer transforms and heals; it instils hope and meaning; it offers a sense of who we are and a vision of who we can be. It is when we ponder the sentiments of prayers such as these in the quiet of our hearts that they become a part of us, influencing our values and actions. Our prayers can then help us to live more wisely and fully as we step beyond our material existence and are reminded of our true spiritual identity.

While the human experience from which a prayer arises is the same, there is a huge variety in the forms of prayer, reflecting the diversity of the cultures, religions and individuals which have produced them. With such a rich heritage of written and spoken prayers, it has been a very hard task to select the few hundred treasures for this anthology. Many are well-known favorites, while others combine deep devotion with a poignancy that breaches the frontiers of religion and culture. Some appeal through their simplicity and directness; others are more elaborate and literary. My aim has been to include a full range of voices: some are well-known religious figures, such as Rúmí and St. Theresa of Ávila, while others may be famous in secular spheres – Beethoven and Michelangelo for example. They are all united by having been touched by the holy, their expression of that experience in turn touching others. Their voices are the reflections of our own struggles and dreams; their prayers are our prayers.

The prayers are organised loosely into sections, purely to help you locate particular types of prayer. You can use this volume as a meditation tool, selecting favorites to include in your daily prayers, or simply browse through at random until a particular prayer inspires you to stop and ponder. Above all we can all glimpse here the glorious technicolor world of humanity's rich diversity, a garden suffused with color and scent. Within these pages, whatever our faith background, we will encounter some new perspective, some different way of expressing a familiar truth, that will delight us, deepen our spiritual insight and, perhaps most importantly, inspire us to strive to realign the spiritual compass of our lives.

JULIET MABEY

BUILDING A
RELATIONSHIP
WITH GOD

Prayer does not change God,
but it changes him who prays.

Søren Kierkegaard

PRAISE AND ADORATION

MY GOD, I love thee; not because
I hope for heaven thereby,
Nor yet because those who love thee not
Are lost eternally.
Not with the hope of gaining aught,
Not seeking a reward;
But as thyself hast loved me,
O ever-loving Lord!
E'en so I love thee, and will love,
And in thy praise will sing,
Solely because thou art my God,
and my eternal King.

ANON

THOU MY mother, and my father thou.
Thou my friend, and my teacher thou.
Thou my wisdom, and my riches thou.
Thou art all to me, O God of all gods.

HINDUISM: Ramanuja

THERE IS a spirit which was before the heavens and the earth
   were.
It is the one dwelling in silence, beyond earthly forms, never
   changing, omnipresent, inexhaustible.
I do not know its name: but if I have to give it a name, I call it
   Tao, I call it the Supreme.
To go to the Supreme is a wandering, a wandering afar, and
   this wandering is a returning.
Man on earth is under the law of the earth. The earth is under
   the law of heaven. Heaven is under the law of Tao. Tao is
   under its own law.

TAOISM

I ADDRESS MYSELF to Thee, Ahura Mazda, to Whom all worship is due. With outstretched arms and open mind and my whole heart, I greet Thee in spirit. Turn Thy countenance towards me, dear Lord, and make my face happy and radiant.

My heart yearns for Thee with a yearning which is never stilled. Thou art my most precious possession, greater and grander, lovelier and dearer by far than the life of my body and the life of my spirit. My joy is in Thee, my refuge is in Thee, my peace is in Thee. Let me live before Thee and with Thee and in Thy sight, I humbly pray.

ZOROASTRIANISM: *The Ahunovati Gatha*

REVERENCING THE Buddha, we offer flowers:
Flowers that today are fresh and sweetly blooming,
Flowers that tomorrow are faded and fallen.
Our bodies too, like flowers, will pass away.

Reverencing the Buddha, we offer candles.
To Him who is the Light, we offer light.
From His greater lamp a lesser lamp we light within us,
The lamp of wisdom shining within our hearts.

Reverencing the Buddha, we offer incense,
Incense whose fragrance pervades the air,
The fragrance of the perfect life, sweeter than incense,
Spreads in all directions throughout the world.

BUDDHISM

I SHALL sing a song of praise to God —
Strike the chords upon the drum.
God who gives us all good things —
Strike the chords upon the drum.
Wives, and wealth, and wisdom —
Strike the chords upon the drum.

AFRICAN TRADITION: *Baluba (Zaire)*

ROUND THY lotus feet, O let my love be wrapt; and it matters
    naught where my body lie,
In city residence or forest hermitage, in rags of poverty, robes
    of wealth:
Teach me but to be faithful unto Thee.
Like the serpent of his gem deprived, so am I in agony without
    a vision of Thee, O Lord.
Let me not by praise or blame be moved: within the depths of
    my soul let me enshrine Thee:
And Thou wilt hold me dear, my Lord!

HINDUISM: *Tulsi Das*

AN EGYPTIAN KING'S HYMN TO ATON (THE SUN)

CREATOR OF the germ in woman,
Maker of seed in man,
Giving life to the son in the body of his mother,
Soothing him that he may not weep,
Nurse (even) in the womb,
Giver of breath to animate every one that he maketh!
When he cometh forth from the womb . . . on the day of his
    birth,
Thou openest his mouth in speech,
Thou suppliest his necessities.
When the fledgling in the egg chirps in the shell
Thou givest him breath therein to preserve him alive . . .
He goeth about upon his two feet
When he hath come forth therefrom.
How manifold are thy works!
They are hidden from before us
O sole God, whose powers no other possesseth.
Thou didst create the earth according to thy heart.

AKHENATON

ALL PRAISE, O my God, be to Thee Who art the Source of all glory and majesty, of greatness and honor, of sovereignty and dominion, of loftiness and grace, of awe and power. Whomsoever Thou willest Thou causest to draw nigh unto the Most Great Ocean, and on whomsoever Thou desirest Thou conferrest the honor of recognizing Thy Most Ancient Name. Of all who are in heaven and on earth, none can withstand the operation of Thy sovereign Will. From all eternity Thou didst rule the entire creation, and Thou wilt continue for evermore to exercise Thy dominion over all created things. There is none other God but Thee, the Almighty, the Most Exalted, the All-Powerful, the All-Wise.

Illumine, O Lord, the faces of Thy servants, that they may behold Thee; and cleanse their hearts that they may turn unto the court of Thy heavenly favors, and recognize Him Who is the Manifestation of Thy Self and the Dayspring of Thine Essence. Verily, Thou art the Lord of all worlds. There is no God but Thee, the Unconstrained, the All-Subduing.

BAHÁ'Í FAITH: *Bahá'u'lláh*

HOW WONDERFUL, O Lord, are the works of your hands!
The heavens declare Your glory,
the arch of sky displays Your handiwork.
In Your love You have given us the power
to behold the beauty of Your world
robed in all its splendor.
The sun and the stars, the valleys and hills,
the rivers and lakes all disclose Your presence.
The roaring breakers of the sea tell of Your awesome might;
the beasts of the field and the birds of the air bespeak Your
        wondrous will.
In Your goodness You have made us able to hear the music of
        the world.
The voices of loved ones reveal to us that You are in our midst.
A divine voice sings through all creation.

JUDAISM

O MY JOY and my Desire and my Refuge,
My Friend and my Sustainer and my Goal;
Thou art my Intimate, and longing for Thee sustains me;
Were it not for Thee, O my Life and my Friend,
How I should have been distraught over the spaces of the
    earth;
How many favors have been bestowed, and how much hast
    Thou given me
Of gifts and grace and assistance;
Thy love is now my desire and my bliss,
And has been revealed to the eye of my heart that was athirst;
I have none beside Thee, Who dost make the desert blossom,
Thou art my joy, firmly established within me;
If Thou art satisfied with me, then,
O Desire of my heart, my happiness has appeared.

ISLAM: *Rábi'a*

O GOD unrecognized, whom all thy works proclaim,
O God, hear these my final words:
If ever I have erred, 'twas searching for thy law;
My heart may go astray, but it is full of thee.

VOLTAIRE

THOU ART the life of the universe; to me
The light of day thou art, and the dark of night:
Activity's field when I do wake and see;
In sleep my dream. Oh, Life of Life, the light
Thou art to me of day, the dark of night.
Relieve me of my vice and virtue;
Make My heart void, and this heart made empty
Fill with thy entirety. Thy excelling take
And make me great with it. Enfold me still
Within thee: cover me, Protector bright,
My light of day who art, and dark of night.

HINDUISM: C. R. Das

O LORD, grant us to love Thee;
    Grant that we may love those that love Thee;
Grant that we may do the deeds that win Thy love.
Make the love of Thee dearer to us than ourselves, than
    our families, than wealth, and even than cool water.

ISLAM: *Ascribed to Muhammad*

ETERNAL GOD,
the light of the minds that know you,
the life of the souls that love you,
the strength of the wills that serve you;
help us so to know you that we may truly love you,
so to love you that we may fully serve you,
whom to serve is perfect freedom.

CHRISTIANITY: *Pope Gelasius' Prayer Book*

L ET US magnify and let us sanctify the great name of God in the world which He created according to His will. May His kingdom come in your lifetime, and in your days, and in the lifetime of the family of Israel – quickly and speedily may it come. Amen.

May the greatness of His being be blessed from eternity to eternity.

Let us bless and let us extol, let us tell aloud and let us raise aloft, let us set on high and let us honor, let us exalt and let us praise the Holy One – blessed be He! – though He is far beyond any blessing or song, any honor or any consolation that can be spoken of in this world. Amen.

May great peace from heaven and the gift of life be granted to us and to all the family of Israel. Amen.

May He who makes peace in the highest bring this peace upon us and upon all Israel. Amen.

JUDAISM: *Kaddish*

MY SOUL hearken unto me!
Love thy Lord as the lotus loves water
Buffeted by waves its affection does not falter.
Creatures that have their being in water,
Taken out of water, die.

My soul if thou hast not such love
How wilt thou obtain release?
If the Word of the Guru is within us
We shall accumulate a store of devotion.

My soul hearken unto me!
Love thy Lord as a fish loves water.
The more the water, the greater its joy,
Greater the tranquility of its body and mind.
Without water it cannot live one watch of the day
Only God knows the anguish of its heart.

My soul hearken unto me!
Love thy Lord as water loves milk.
It takes on the heat, boils and evaporates before the milk can
    suffer.
He alone unites, He alone separates,
He alone bestows true greatness.

Without the Guru, love cannot be born
The dross of ego cannot be rinsed away.
He who recognizes the God within
Understands the secret of the Word and is happy.
O Nanak! there is but one gate to the Lord's mansion
And there is no other sanctuary.

SIKHISM

LATE HAVE I loved Thee, O Beauty so ancient and so new; late have I loved Thee: for behold Thou wert within me, and I outside; and I sought Thee outside and in my unloveliness fell upon those lovely things that Thou has made. Thou wert with me, and I was not with Thee. I was kept from Thee by those things, yet had they not been in Thee, they would not have been at all. Thou didst call and cry to me to break open my deafness: and Thou didst send forth Thy beams and shine upon me and chase away my blindness: Thou didst breathe fragrance upon me, and I drew in my breath and do now pant for Thee: I tasted Thee, and now hunger and thirst for Thee: Thou didst touch me, and I have burned for Thy peace.

CHRISTIANITY: *St. Augustine*

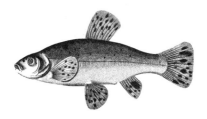

THANKSGIVING

LISTEN, O fortunate ones, to my joyful song,
That all my desires have been fulfilled.
I have obtained God, the Supreme Being,
And all my griefs have disappeared.
My sorrows, afflictions, and sufferings have departed
By listening to the true Word.
The saints and the holy are filled with joy,
When they hear the Word from the perfect Preceptor.
He who hears the Word is made pure,
He who speaks is made holy,
The Eternal Preceptor will fill their hearts.
I proclaim, for those who attach themselves to the
     Enlightener's feet,
The heavenly music plays.

SIKHISM: *Japji*

WE RETURN thanks to our mother, the earth, which sustains us.

We return thanks to the rivers and streams, which supply us with water.

We return thanks to all herbs, which furnish medicines for the cure of our diseases.

We return thanks to the corn, and to her sisters, the beans and squashes, which give us life.

We return thanks to the bushes and trees, which provide us with fruit.

We return thanks to the wind, which, moving the air, has banished diseases.

We return thanks to the moon and stars, which give us their light when the sun has gone.

We return thanks to our grandfather, He'no, that he has protected his grandchildren from witches and reptiles, and has given to us his rain.

We return thanks to the sun, that he has looked upon the earth with a beneficent eye.

Lastly, we return thanks to the Great Spirit, in whom is embodied all goodness, and who directs all things for the good of his children.

NATIVE AMERICAN TRADITION: *Iroquois*

I THANK YOU, Lord, for knowing me better than I know myself, and for letting me know myself better than others know me. Make me, I pray to You, better than they suppose, and forgive me for what they do not know.

ISLAM: Abu Bakr

H ELP US to look back on the long way that Thou hast brought us, on the long days in which we have been served not according to our deserts but our desires; on the pit and the miry clay, the blackness of despair, the horror of misconduct, from which our feet have been plucked out.

For our sins forgiven or prevented, for our shame unpublished, we bless and thank Thee, O God. Help us yet again and ever. So order events, so strengthen our frailty, as that day by day we shall come before Thee with this song of gratitude, and in the end we be dismissed with honour. In their weakness and fear, the vessels of thy handiwork so pray to Thee, so praise Thee.

ROBERT LOUIS STEVENSON

O LORD, fill us, we beseech You, with adoring gratitude to You for all You are for us, to us, and in us; fill us with love, joy, peace, and all the fruits of the Spirit.

CHRISTINA ROSSETTI

O MY father, Great Elder,
I have no words to thank you,
But with your deep wisdom
I am sure that you can see
How I value your glorious gifts.
O my Father, when I look upon your greatness,
I am confounded with awe.
O Great Elder,
Ruler of all things earthly and heavenly,
I am your warrior,
Ready to act in accordance with your will.

AFRICAN TRADITION: *Kikuyu (Kenya)*

i thank You God for most this amazing
day:for the leaping greenly spirits of trees
and a blue true dream of sky;and for everything
which is natural which is infinite which is yes

(i who have died am alive again today,
this is the suns birthday;this is the birth
day of life and of love and of wings:and of the gay
great happening illimitably earth)

how should tasting touching hearing seeing
breathing any – lifted from the no
of all nothing – human merely being
doubt unimaginable You?

(now the ears of my ears awake and
now the eyes of my eyes are opened)

E. E. CUMMINGS

M Y GOD, my Adored One, my King, my Desire! What tongue can voice my thanks to Thee? I was heedless, Thou didst awaken me. I had turned back from Thee, Thou didst graciously aid me to turn towards Thee. I was as one dead. Thou didst quicken me with the water of life. I was withered, Thou didst revive me with the heavenly stream of Thine utterance which hath flowed forth from the Pen of the All-Merciful.

O Divine Providence! All existence is begotten by Thy bounty; deprive it not of the waters of Thy generosity, neither do Thou withhold it from the ocean of Thy mercy. I beseech Thee to aid and assist me at all times and under all conditions, and seek from the heaven of Thy grace Thine ancient favor. Thou art, in truth, the Lord of bounty, and the Sovereign of the kingdom of eternity.

BAHÁ'Í FAITH: *Bahá'u'lláh*

O GOD, I thank Thee for all the joy I have had in life.

EARL BRIHTNOTH

FOR FLOWERS that bloom about our feet;
For tender grass, so fresh and sweet;
For song of bird and hum of bee;
For all things fair we hear or see
Father in Heaven, we thank Thee!

For blue of stream, for blue of sky;
For pleasant shade of branches high;
For fragrant air and cooling breeze;
For beauty of the blowing trees –
Father in Heaven, we thank Thee!
For mother-love, for father-care;
For brothers strong and sisters fair;
For love at home and school each day;
for guidance lest we go astray –
Father in Heaven, we thank Thee!

For Thy dear, everlasting arms,
That bear us o'er all ills and harms;
For blessed words of long ago,
That help us now Thy will to know –
Father in Heaven, we thank Thee!

RALPH WALDO EMERSON

THANKS BE to thee,
Lord Jesus Christ,
for all the benefits
which thou hast given us,
for all the pains and insults
which thou hast borne for us.

O most merciful redeemer, friend and brother,
may we know thee more clearly,
love thee more dearly,
and follow thee more nearly,
day by day.

CHRISTIANITY: *Richard of Chichester*

SEEKING NEARNESS TO GOD

Y OU WILL seek me and find me when you seek me with all
your heart.

JUDAISM: *Jeremiah 29*

LORD, WE are rivers running to thy sea,
Our waves and ripples all derived from thee:
A nothing we should have, a nothing be,
    Except for thee.

Sweet are the waters of thy shoreless sea,
Make sweet our waters that make haste to thee;
Pour in thy sweetness, that ourselves may be
    Sweetness to thee.

CHRISTINA ROSSETTI

GOD BE in my head
   and in my understanding;
God be in my eyes
   and in my looking;
God be in my mouth
   and in my speaking;
God be in my heart
   and in my thinking;
God be at my end
   and at my departing.

CHRISTIANITY: *Book of Hours*

REVEAL THYSELF to me, reveal thyself to me.
I seek not wealth nor power, I yearn to see thee alone.
O God, I care not for renunciation or enjoyment, I yearn to see
   thee alone.
O God, I am neither anxious for home, nor for the forest of life;
I only yearn to see thee.
Yea I seek for nought save thee, O God, I yearn for thy vision
   alone; grant my prayer.

HINDUISM: *Dadu*

O MY GOD, how great is my desire to meet with Thee and how great is my hope of Thy reward. Thou art gracious, there is no disappointment from Thee, the Hope of all who hope; there is no frustration with Thee, Thou Desire of all who yearn. O my God, if I am unworthy of Thee and my works do not bring me near unto Thee, yet my weakness has made confession of my sins, and if Thou dost forgive – Who has more power to forgive than Thyself, and if Thou dost punish Who is more just to perform it than Thyself? O my Lord, my tears have flowed for my soul in looking upon her, but there remains for her the beauty of looking upon Thee, and woe be to my soul if she rejoices not therein. O my God, let not faith fail me all the days of my life, nor cut off from me Thy benevolence after my death. I have hoped that He Whose goodness has followed me all the days of my life will be near me with His pardon at the hour of death. O my Lord, how should I despair of the beauty of the Vision of Thyself after my death, when Thou hast bestowed upon me nought but good in my lifetime? O God, if my sins have made me afraid, verily my love to Thee has protected me (or brought me near unto Thee). O my Lord, if it were not for the sins I have committed, I would not have feared Thy chastisement, and if I had not known Thy grace, I should not have hoped for Thy reward.

ISLAM: *Sha'wána*

Seeking Nearness to God ⟿ 35

HERE IN the maddening maze of things,
When tossed by storm or flood,
To one fixed ground my spirit clings,
I know that God is good.

I know not what the future hath,
Of marvel or surprise,
Assured alone that life and death,
His mercy underlies.

I know not where his islands lift,
Their fronded palms in air,
I only know I cannot drift,
Beyond His love and care.

JOHN GREENLEAF WHITTIER

O LET ME behold Thee in every place! When I feel myself
inflamed by mortal beauty, my ardour for Thy beauty is
extinguished and I am enkindled by it as formerly I was by
Thine. O my true Lord, to Thee alone I call for help against my
blind, useless torment, for Thou alone canst inwardly and
outwardly renew my senses, will and power which are weak and
languid.

MICHELANGELO

FORTH IN your name, O Lord, I go,
my daily labour to pursue,
you, only you, resolved to know
in all I think, or speak or do.

The task your wisdom has assigned
O let me cheerfully fulfil,
in all my works your presence find,
and prove your good and perfect will.

CHRISTIANITY: Charles Wesley

O GOD, let our tongues be refreshed with the remembrance of Thee, our souls obedient to Thy command, our hearts filled with the knowledge of Thee, our spirits sanctified with the vision of Thee, and our secret selves graced by nearness to Thee . . .

O God, no heart is at rest except close to Thee, no servant lives except by Thy gentleness and kindly grace. There is no continuing to be unless Thy decree be so. O Thou who in tenderness hast graced the righteous and the blessed in their access to Thy presence so that salvation is theirs and the knowledge of Thy mysteries, O my Lord, what door shall I seek out unless it be Thine? To whose court shall I repair if not to Thine?

ISLAM: Al-Fuyúdat al-Rabbániyyah

LORD, THOU mighty River, all-knowing, all-seeing,
And I like a little fish in Thy great waters,
How shall I sound Thy depths?
How shall I reach Thy shores?
Wherever I go, I see Thee only,
And snatched out of Thy waters, I die of separation.
I know not the fisher, I see not the net,
But flapping in my agony I call upon Thee for help.
O Lord who pervades all things,
In my folly I thought Thee far,
But no deed I do can ever be out of thy sight.

SIKHISM: *Guru Nanak*

O MY GOD, the best of Thy gifts within my heart is the hope of Thee and the sweetest word upon my tongue is Thy praise, and the hours which I love best are those in which I meet with Thee. O my God, I cannot endure without the remembrance of Thee in this world and how shall I be able to endure without the vision of Thee in the next world? O my Lord, my plaint to Thee is that I am but a stranger in Thy country, and lonely among Thy worshippers.

ISLAM: *Rábi'a*

O THOU WHOSE nearness is my wish, Whose presence is my hope, Whose remembrance is my desire, Whose court of glory is my goal, Whose abode is my aim, Whose name is my healing, Whose love is the radiance of my heart, Whose service is my highest aspiration! I beseech Thee by Thy Name, through which Thou hast enabled them that have recognized Thee to soar to the sublimest heights of the knowledge of Thee and empowered such as devoutly worship Thee to ascend into the precincts of the court of Thy holy favors, to aid me to turn my face towards Thy face, to fix mine eyes upon Thee, and to speak of Thy glory.

I am the one, O my Lord, who hath forgotten all else but Thee, and turned towards the Dayspring of Thy grace, who hath forsaken all save Thyself in the hope of drawing nigh unto Thy court. Behold me, then, with mine eyes lifted up toward the Seat that shineth with the splendors of the light of Thy Face. Send down, then, upon me, O my Beloved, that which will enable me to be steadfast in Thy Cause, so that the doubts of the infidels may not hinder me from turning toward Thee.

Thou art, verily, the God of Power, the Help in Peril, the All-Glorious, the Almighty.

BAHÁ'Í FAITH: *Bahá'u'lláh*

BE THOU my vision, O Lord of my heart,
Be all else but naught to me, save that thou art;
Be thou my best thought in the day and the night,
Both waking and sleeping, thy presence my light.

Be thou my wisdom, be thou my true word;
Be thou ever with me, and I with thee, Lord;
Be thou my great Father, and I thy true son;
Be thou in me dwelling, and I with thee one.

Be thou and thou only the first in my heart;
O Sovereign of heaven, my treasure thou art;
Great Heart of my own heart, whatever befall,
Still be thou my vision, O Ruler of all.

CELTIC PRAYER

NO SEPARATION exists between the Beloved and the lover.
I do not belong to myself. I am His possession.

ISLAM: *Rábi'a*

O THOU
who hast given me eyes
to see the light
that fills my room,
give me the inward vision
to behold thee in this place.

O Thou
who hast made me to feel
the morning wind upon my limbs,
help me to feel thy Presence
as I bow in worship of thee.

HINDUISM: *Chandra Devanesen*

TEACH ME, my God and King,
in all things thee to see,
and what I do in anything
to do it as for thee.

GEORGE HERBERT

IN THY image let me pattern my life, O Ahura Mazda,
Let me awake with Thy name on my lips
In my eyes let me ever carry thy image
To enable me to perceive Thee,
And Thee alone, in everyone else.

ZOROASTRIANISM

MAY ALL I say and all I think
Be in harmony with thee,
God within me,
God beyond me,
maker of the trees.

NATIVE AMERICAN TRADITION: *Chinook*

SPIRITUAL ENRICHMENT

G UIDE US, teach us, and strengthen us, O Lord, we beseech Thee, until we become such as Thou wouldest have us be; pure, gentle, truthful, high-minded, courteous, generous, able, dutiful and useful; for Thy honour and glory.

CHARLES KINGSLEY

I PRAY THEE, Lord, let my way be resolute and my purpose firm in thy good counsel. Grant me, O Lord, the boon of gratefulness for thy grace, the beauty that belongs with thy worship. Give me a pure and reverent heart, uprightness of character, a tongue that speaks right and deeds that are worthy, O Lord God.

ISLAM: *Al-Ghazzálí*

LIVING BEINGS are without number: I vow to row them to the other shore.
Defilements are without number: I vow to remove them from myself.
The teachings are immeasurable: I vow to study and practice them.
The way is very long: I vow to arrive at the end.

MAHAYANA BUDDHISM: *The Vow of the Bodhisattva*

INCLINE US, O God,
to think humbly of ourselves,
to be saved only in the examination of our own conduct,
to consider our fellow-creatures with kindness,
and to judge of all they say and do with the charity
which we would desire from them ourselves.

JANE AUSTEN

TAKE AWAY out of our hearts, O Lord God, all self-confidence and boasting, all high and vain thoughts, all desire to excuse ourselves for our sins or to compare ourselves proudly with others; and grant us rather to take as master and King him who chose to be crowned with thorns and to die in shame for others and for us all, thy Son our Saviour Jesus Christ.

DEAN VAUGHAN

MAY I REACH

That purest heaven, be to other souls
The cup of strength in some great agony,
Enkindle generous ardour, feed pure love,
Be the sweet presence of a good diffused,
And in diffusion ever more intense!
So shall I join the choir invisible
Whose music is the gladness of the world.

GEORGE ELIOT

DEAR AHURA Mazda, men in this world claim greatness for many a varied reason but the truly great man in Thine eyes is the one who is wholly righteous, who has acquired an insight into Thy Law of Righteousness and who guides and helps others along its path. Thy gift of Divine Wisdom is vouchsafed unto them who serve Thy cause and purpose in life. Thy very strength and power are reserved for those who succor the poor and lowly. For righteousness is the highest blessing which Thou, Ahura Mazda, hast bestowed upon man.

ZOROASTRIANISM

THIS IS my prayer to thee, my lord –
    strike, strike at the root of penury in my heart.
Give me the strength lightly to bear my joys and sorrows.
Give me the strength to make my love fruitful in service.
Give me the strength never to disown the poor or bend my
    knees before insolent might.
Give me the strength to raise my mind high above daily trifles.
And give me the strength to surrender my strength to thy will
    with love.

HINDUISM: Rabindranath Tagore

O KIND FATHER, loving Father, through Thy mercy we have spent our day in peace and happiness; grant that we may, according to Thy will, do what is right.

Give us light, give us understanding, so that we may know what pleases Thee.

We offer this prayer in Thy presence, O wonderful Lord:

Forgive us our sins. Help us in keeping ourselves pure. Bring us into the fellowship of those in whose company we may remember Thy name.

[Through Nanak] may Thy name forever be on the increase, and may all men prosper by Thy grace.

SIKHISM: Guru Gobind Singh

O GOD, our Father, help us all through this day so to live that we may bring help to others, credit to ourselves and to the name we bear, and joy to those that love us, and to you.

Enable us to be:

    Cheerful when things go wrong;

    Persevering when things are difficult;

    Serene when things are irritating;

    Helpful to those in difficulties;

    Kind to those in need;

    Sympathetic to those whose hearts are sore and sad.

Grant that:

    Nothing may make us lose our tempers;

    Nothing may take away our joy;

    Nothing may ruffle our peace;

    Nothing may make us bitter towards anyone.

So grant that through all this day all with whom we work, and all those whom we meet, may see in us the reflection of the master, whose we are and whom we seek to serve. This we ask for your love's sake.

WILLIAM BARCLAY

O LORD, I place myself in your hands and dedicate myself to
   you.
I pledge myself to do your will in all things –
To love the Lord God with all my heart, all my soul, all my
   strength.
Not to kill, not to steal, not to covet, not to bear false witness,
   to honor all persons.
Not to do to another what I should not want done to myself.
To chastise the body. Not to seek after pleasures. To love
   fasting. To relieve the poor.
To clothe the naked. To visit the sick. To bury the dead.
To help in trouble. To console the sorrowing.
To hold myself aloof from worldly ways.
To prefer nothing to the love of Christ.
Not to give way to anger. Not to foster a desire for revenge.
Not to entertain deceit in the heart. Not to make a false peace.
Not to forsake charity.
Not to swear, lest I swear falsely.
To speak the truth with heart and tongue.
Not to return evil for evil.
To do no injury, indeed, even to bear patiently any injury
   done to me.
To love my enemies. Not to curse those who curse me but
   rather to bless them.

To bear persecution for justice's sake.

Not to be proud.

Not to be given to intoxicating drink. Not to be an overeater.

Not to be lazy. Not to be slothful.

Not to be a murmurer. Not to be a detractor.

To put my trust in God.

To refer the good I see in myself to God.

To refer any evil I see in myself to myself.

To fear the day of judgment. To be in dread of hell.

To desire eternal life with spiritual longing.

To keep death before my eyes daily.

To keep constant watch over my actions.

To remember that God sees me everywhere.

To call upon Christ for defense against evil thoughts that arise in my heart.

To guard my tongue against wicked speech.

To avoid much speaking. To avoid idle talk.

Not to seek to appear clever.

To read only what is good to read.

To pray often.

To ask forgiveness daily for my sins, and to seek ways to amend my life.

To obey my superiors in all things rightful.

Not to desire to be thought holy, but to seek holiness.

To fulfill the commandments of God by good works.

To love chastity. To hate no one. Not be jealous or envious of anyone.

Not to love strife. Not to love pride.

To honor the aged. To pray for my enemies.

To make peace after a quarrel, before the setting of the sun.

Never to despair of your mercy, O God of Mercy.

CHRISTIANITY: St. Benedict

OUR EYES may see some uncleanness, but let not our mind see things that are not clean.

Our ears may hear some uncleanness, but let not our mind hear things that are not clean.

SHINTO

GLORIOUS GOD, give me grace to amend my life, and to have an eye to my end without begrudging death, which to those who die in you, good Lord, is the gate of a wealthy life.

And give me, good Lord, a humble, lowly, quiet, peaceable, patient, charitable, kind, tender and pitiful mind, in all my works and all my words and all my thoughts, to have a taste of your holy, blessed Spirit.

Give me, good Lord, a full faith, a firm hope, and a fervent charity, a love of you incomparably above the love of myself.

Give me, good Lord, a longing to be with you, not to avoid the calamities of this world, nor so much to attain the joys of heaven, as simply for love of you.

And give me, good Lord, your love and favor, which my love of you, however great it might be, could not deserve were it not for your great goodness.

These things, good Lord, that I pray for, give me your grace to labor for.

CHRISTIANITY: *Sir Thomas More*

O GREAT SPIRIT, whose voice speaks in the wind,
whose breath gives life to all the world.
Hear me!
I am small and weak, I need your power and wisdom.
Let me walk in beauty, and let my eyes be glad
beholding the red and golden dawn.
Make my hands touch all things
you have made with love.
Make me wise that I may understand
the sacred teachings you have taught.
Help me learn the lessons hidden
in every leaf and every stone.
I seek strength, not to be greater than my brother
but to conquer the enemy in myself.
Make me ready to come to you always
with a pure heart and with clear eyes,
so when my life fades away, like the setting sun,
my spirit may come to you
with honor and without shame.

NATIVE AMERICAN TRADITION: *Dakota*

FAITH AND STEADFASTNESS

GIVE ME, O Lord, a steadfast heart,
    which no unworthy affection may drag downwards;
    give me an unconquered heart,
    which no tribulation can wear out;
    give me an upright heart,
    which no unworthy purpose may tempt aside.
    Bestow on me also, O Lord, my God,
    understanding to know you,
    diligence to seek you,
    wisdom to find you,
    and a faithfulness that may finally embrace you,
    through Jesus Christ our Lord, Amen.

CHRISTIANITY: *St. Thomas Aquinas*

WHEN ALL within is dark,
and former friends misprise;
from them I turn to you,
and find love in Your eyes.

When all within is dark,
and I my soul despise;
from me I turn to You,
and find love in Your eyes.

When all Your face is dark,
and Your just angers rise;
From You I turn to You,
and find love in Your eyes.

ISRAEL ABRAHAMS, *based on Ibn Gabirol*

O MERCIFUL GOD, be Thou now unto me a strong tower of defense, I humbly entreat Thee. Give me grace to await Thy leisure, and patiently to bear what Thou doest unto me; nothing doubting or mistrusting Thy goodness towards me; for Thou knowest what is good for me better than I do.

Therefore do with me in all things that Thou wilt; only arm me, I beseech Thee, with Thine armor, that I may stand fast, above all things, taking to me the shield of faith; praying always that I may refer myself wholly to Thy will, abiding Thy pleasure, and comforting myself in those troubles which it shall please Thee to send me, seeing such troubles are profitable for me; and I am assuredly persuaded that all Thou doest cannot but be well; and unto Thee be all honor and glory. Amen.

LADY JANE GREY, *on the eve of her execution*

GRANT ME, O Master, by thy grace
To follow all the good and pure;
To be content with simple things;
To speak no ill of others;
To have a mind at peace;
Set free from care, and led astray from thee,
Neither by happiness nor woe;
To consider my fellows not as means but ends,
To serve them stalwartly in thought, word and deed;
Never to utter a word of hatred or of shame;
To cast away all selfishness and pride.

Set thou my feet upon this path,
And keep me steadfast in it:
Thus only shall I please thee, serve thee right.

HINDUISM: *Tulsi Das*

GOD, OUR Father, we are exceedingly frail and indisposed to every virtuous and gallant undertaking. Strengthen our weakness, we beseech you, that we may do valiantly in this spiritual war; help us against our own negligence and cowardice, and defend us from the treachery of our unfaithful hearts; for Jesus Christ's sake.

CHRISTIANITY: *Thomas à Kempis*

O LORD, MY God! Assist Thy loved ones to be firm in Thy Faith, to walk in Thy ways, to be steadfast in Thy Cause. Give them Thy grace to withstand the onslaught of self and passion, to follow the light of divine guidance. Thou art the Powerful, the Gracious, the Self-Subsisting, the Bestower, the Compassionate, the Almighty, the All-Bountiful.

BAHÁ'Í FAITH: *'Abdu'l-Bahá*

O GOD, GIVE me light in my heart and light in my tongue and light in my hearing and light in my sight and light in my feeling and light in all my body and light before me and light behind me.

Give me, I pray Thee, light on my right hand and light on my left hand and light above me and light beneath me, O Lord, increase light within me and give me light and illuminate me.

ISLAM: *Ascribed to Muhammad*

F IX THOU our steps, O Lord, that we stagger not at the uneven motions of the world, but steadily go on to our glorious home; neither censuring our journey by the weather we meet with, nor turning out of the way for anything that befalls us.

The winds are often rough, and our own weight presses us downwards. Reach forth, O Lord, thy hand, thy saving hand, and speedily deliver us.

Teach us, O Lord, to use this transitory life as pilgrims returning to their beloved home; that we may take what our journey requires, and not think of settling in a foreign country.

CHRISTIANITY: *John Wesley*

O GOD, WHO art rich and praiseworthy, who createst and restorest to life, who art merciful and loving, make me to abound in what is lawful in thy sight, in obedience to thee and by grace from thee, so that I turn from what is unlawful, from disobedience and from all other than thou.

ISLAM: *Al-Ghazzálí*

A STRONG FAITH

BEHOLD, LORD, an empty vessel that needs to be filled. My Lord, fill it. I am weak in the faith; strengthen thou me. I am cold in love; warm me and make me fervent that my love may go out to my neighbor. I do not have a strong and firm faith; at times I doubt and am unable to trust thee altogether. O Lord, help me. Strengthen my faith and trust in thee. In thee I have sealed the treasures of all I have. I am poor; thou art rich and didst come to be merciful to the poor. I am a sinner; thou art upright. With me there is an abundance of sin; in thee is the fullness of righteousness. Therefore, I will remain with thee of whom I can receive but to whom I may not give.

CHRISTIANITY: *Martin Luther*

MAKE FIRM our steps, O Lord, in Thy path and strengthen Thou our hearts in Thine obedience. Turn our faces toward the beauty of Thy oneness, and gladden our bosoms with the signs of Thy divine unity. Adorn our bodies with the robe of Thy bounty, and remove from our eyes the veil of sinfulness, and give us the chalice of Thy grace; that the essence of all beings may sing Thy praise before the vision of Thy grandeur. Reveal then Thyself, O Lord, by Thy merciful utterance and the mystery of Thy divine being, that the holy ecstasy of prayer may fill our souls – a prayer that shall rise above words and letters and transcend the murmur of syllables and sounds – that all things may be merged into nothingness before the revelation of Thy splendor.

Lord! These are servants that have remained fast and firm in Thy Covenant and Thy Testament, that have held fast unto the cord of constancy in Thy Cause and clung unto the hem of the robe of Thy grandeur. Assist them, O Lord, with Thy grace, confirm with Thy power and strengthen their loins in obedience to Thee.

Thou art the Pardoner, the Gracious.

BAHÁ'Í FAITH: *'Abdu'l-Bahá*

SELF-FORGETFULNESS

O GOD, HELP me to have victory over myself, for it is difficult to conquer oneself, though when that is conquered, all is conquered.

JAIN SCRIPTURES

L ORD, ENFOLD me in the depths of your heart; and there hold me, refine, purge, and set me on fire, raise me aloft, until my own self knows utter annihilation.

PIERRE TEILHARD DE CHARDIN

TAKE LORD, unto Thyself,
My sense of self and let it vanish utterly.

Take Lord, my life,
Live Thou Thy life through me.

I live no longer Lord,
But in me now
Thou livest.

Aye, between Thee and me my God.
There is no longer room for "I" and "mine".

HINDUISM: *Tukaram*

TO THEE, O Jesu, I direct my eyes;
to thee my hands, to thee my humble knees;
to thee my heart shall offer sacrifice;
to thee my thoughts, who my thoughts only sees;
to thee my self – my self and all I give;
to thee I die;
to thee I only live.

SIR WALTER RALEIGH

LORD JESUS,
I give thee my hands to do thy work.
I give thee my feet to go thy way.
I give thee my eyes to see as thou seest.
I give thee my tongue to speak thy words.
I give thee my mind that thou mayest think in me.
I give thee my spirit that thou mayest pray in me.
Above all, I give thee my heart that thou mayest
    love in me
    thy Father, and all mankind.
I give thee my whole self, that thou mayest grow in me, so
      that it is thee, Lord Jesus, who lives and works and prays
      in me.
I hand over to thy care, Lord,
    my soul and body,
    my prayers and my hopes,
    my health and my work,
    my life and my death,
    my parents and my family,
    my friends and my neighbors,
    my country and all men,
    today and always.

CHRISTIANITY: *Bishop Lancelot Andrewes*

MAY I become a medicine for the sick and their physician, their
support until sickness come not again.

May I become an unfailing store for the wretched, and be first
to supply them with their needs.

My own self and my pleasures, my righteousness past, present,
and future, may I sacrifice without regard, in order to
achieve the welfare of beings.

MAHAYANA BUDDHISM: *Santideva*

O LORD! Unto Thee I repair for refuge, and toward all Thy
signs I set my heart.

O Lord! Whether traveling or at home, and in my
occupation or in my work, I place my whole trust in Thee.

Grant me then Thy sufficing help so as to make me
independent of all things, O Thou Who art unsurpassed in Thy
mercy!

Bestow upon me my portion, O Lord, as Thou pleasest, and
cause me to be satisfied with whatsoever Thou hast ordained
for me.

Thine is the absolute authority to command.

BAHÁ'Í FAITH: *The Báb*

I HAVE set God always before me:
because he is on my right hand,
I shall not fall.

JUDAISM: *Psalm 16.9*

SEVER ME from myself that I may be grateful unto thee;
May I perish to myself that I may be safe in thee;
May I die to myself that I may live in thee;
May I wither to myself that I may blossom in thee;
May I be emptied of myself that I may abound in thee;
May I be nothing to myself that I may be all to thee.

CHRISTIANITY: *Desiderius Erasmus*

SERENELY I will submit to all changes and I will put my whole confidence, O God, only in Thy unchangeable goodness.

LUDWIG VAN BEETHOVEN

MAY THE passions of lust, anger, greed, pride and attachment depart from me. O Lord, I come to seek Thy shelter. Bless me with thy grace.

SIKHISM: *Sacred Song*

LORD, MAKE me according to thy heart.

CHRISTIANITY: *Brother Lawrence*

LORD, MAKE me like crystal that your light may shine through me.

KATHERINE MANSFIELD

ONLY LET me make my life simple and straight like a flute of reed for Thee to fill with music.

ANON

DEAREST LORD, teach me to be generous;
Teach me to serve thee as thou deservest;
To give and not to count the cost,
To fight and not to heed the wounds,
To toil and not to seek for rest,
To labor and not to seek reward,
Save that of knowing that I do thy will.

CHRISTIANITY: *St. Ignatius Loyola*

O LORD GOD, thou knowest my secret and my open things: receive my plea. Thou knowest my need. Grant, therefore, my petition. Thou knowest all that is in my soul.

O Lord God, I ask of thee a faith to occupy my heart and a true assurance, whereby I may know that nought shall ever befall me outside thy purposed will for me. Let me be well pleased with whatever thou allottest me, O thou Lord of majesty and honor.

ISLAM: *Al-Ghazzálí*

TO LORD KRISHNA

EVERY THOUGHT of my mind,
every emotion of my heart,
every movement of my being,
every feeling and every sensation,
each cell of my body, each drop of my blood
– all, all is yours,
yours absolutely,
yours without reserve,
you can decide my life or my death,
my happiness or my sorrow,
my pleasure or my pain.
Whatever you do with me,
whatever comes to me from you,
will lead me to the Divine Rapture.

HINDUISM: *Bhagavata Purana*

INNER PEACE
AND TRANQUILITY

GOD GRANT me the serenity to accept the things that cannot be
   changed; courage to change the things I can; and wisdom
   to know the difference.
Living one day at a time;
Enjoying one moment at a time;
Accepting hardships as the pathway to peace;
Taking this sinful world as it is, not as I would have it;
Trusting that you will make all things right if I surrender to your will;
That I may be reasonably happy in this life
And supremely happy with you forever in the next.

REINHOLD NIEBUHR

THE LORD bless you
   and keep you;
the Lord make his face shine upon you
   and be gracious to you;
the Lord turn his face towards you
   and give you peace.

JUDAISM: *Numbers 6.24–6*

G RANT ME, O Lord, the royalty of inward happiness and the serenity which comes from living close to thee. Daily renew the sense of joy, and let the eternal spirit of the Father dwell in my soul and body, filling every corner of my heart with light and grace, so that bearing about with me the infection of a good courage, I may be a diffuser of life and may meet all ills and crosses with gallant and high-hearted happiness, giving thee thanks always for all things.

ROBERT LOUIS STEVENSON

CREATE IN me a pure heart, O my God, and renew a tranquil conscience within me, O my Hope! Through the spirit of power confirm Thou me in Thy Cause, O my Best-Beloved, and by the light of Thy glory reveal unto me Thy path, O Thou the Goal of my desire! Through the power of Thy transcendent might lift me unto the heaven of Thy holiness, O Source of my being, and by the breezes of Thine eternity gladden me, O Thou Who art my God! Let Thine everlasting melodies breathe tranquility on me, O my Companion, and let the riches of Thine ancient countenance deliver me from all except Thee, O my Master, and let the tidings of the revelation of Thine incorruptible Essence bring me joy, O Thou Who art the most manifest of the manifest and the most hidden of the hidden!

BAHÁ'Í FAITH: *Bahá'u'lláh*

DROP THY still dews of quietness,
Till all our strivings cease;
Take from our souls the strain and stress,
And let our ordered lives confess
The beauty of thy peace.

JOHN GREENLEAF WHITTIER

OUR GOD, bestow upon us such confidence, such peace, such happiness in Thee, that Thy will may always be dearer to us than our own will, and Thy pleasure than our own pleasure. All that Thou givest is Thy free gift to us, all that Thou takest away is Thy grace to us. Be Thou thanked for all, praised for all, loved for all; through Jesus Christ our Lord.

CHRISTINA ROSSETTI

DEEP PEACE of the running wave to you,
Deep peace of the flowing air to you,
Deep peace of the quiet earth to you,
Deep peace of the shining stars to you,
Deep peace of the Son of Peace to you.

CELTIC PRAYER

O LORD, CALM the waves of this heart; calm its tempests. Calm thyself, O my soul, so that the divine can act in thee. Calm thyself, O my soul, so that God is able to repose in thee, so that his peace may cover thee. Yes, Father in heaven, often have we found that the world cannot give us peace, O but make us feel that thou art able to give peace; let us know the truth of thy promise: that the whole world may not be able to take away thy peace.

SØREN KIERKEGAARD

HAVE NO anxiety at all,
But in everything,
By prayer and petition,
With thanksgiving,
Let your requests be known to God.
Then the peace of God that
Surpasses all understanding
Will fill your heart and
Your mind
In Christ Jesus

CHRISTIANITY: *Philippians 4.6–7*

MAY EVERY creature abound in well-being and peace.
May every living being, weak or strong, the long and the small,
The short and the medium-sized, the mean and the great,
May every living being, seen or unseen, those dwelling far off,
Those near by, those already born, those waiting to be born,
May all attain inward peace.

Let no one deceive another,
Let no one despise another in any situation,
Let no one, from antipathy or hatred, wish evil to anyone.
Just as a mother, with her own life, protects her only son from
    hurt,
So within yourself foster a limitless concern for every living
    creature.
Display a heart of boundless love for all the world
In all its height and depth and broad extent,
Love unrestrained, without hate or enmity.
Then as you stand or walk, sit or lie, until overcome by
    drowsiness,
Devote your mind entirely to this, it is known as living here
    life divine.

BUDDHISM

AID AND ASSISTANCE IN TIMES OF NEED

Do not be far from me,
For trouble is near
And there is no one to help.

PSALM 22.11

COMFORT AND STRENGTH

THE LORD is my shepherd, I shall not want. He maketh me to lie down in green pastures, he leadeth me beside the still waters, he restoreth my soul.

He leadeth me in the paths of righteousness for his name's sake.

Even though I walk through the valley of the shadow of death, I will fear no evil: for thou art with me; thy rod and thy staff they comfort me.

Thou preparest a table before me in the presence of mine enemies: thou anointest my head with oil; my cup runneth over.

Surely goodness and mercy shall follow me all the days of my life: and I will dwell in the house of the Lord for ever.

JUDAISM: *Psalm 23*

O BLESSED JESUS Christ, who didst bid all who carry heavy burdens to come to thee, refresh us with thy presence and thy power. Quiet our understandings and give ease to our hearts, by bringing us close to things infinite and eternal. Open to us the mind of God, that in his light we may see light. And crown thy choice of us to be thy servants, by making us springs of strength and joy to all whom we serve.

EVELYN UNDERHILL

O OUR FATHER, the Sky, hear us and make us strong.
O our Mother the Earth, hear us and give us support.
O Spirit of the East, send us your wisdom.
O Spirit of the South, may we tread your path of life.
O Spirit of the West, may we always be ready for the long
    journey.
O Spirit of the North, purify us with your cleansing winds.

NATIVE AMERICAN TRADITION: *Sioux*

HE WHO calls to God from the depths of his heart, will find his abode in the clear skies of love.

SUFISM: *Ali Nader*

Comfort and Strength 77

ON ANOTHER'S SORROW

CAN I SEE another's woe,
And not be in sorrow too?
Can I see another's grief,
And not seek for kind relief?

Can I see a falling tear,
And not feel my sorrow's share?
Can a father see his child
Weep, nor be with sorrow fill'd?

Can a mother sit and hear
An infant groan an infant fear?
No, no, never can it be!
Never, never can it be!

And can he who smiles on all
Hear the wren with sorrows small,
Hear the small bird's grief and care,
Hear the woes that infants bear,

And not sit beside the nest,
Pouring pity in their breast;

And not sit the cradle near,
Weeping tear on infant's tear.

And not sit both night and day,
Wiping all our tears away?
O, no! never can it be!
Never, never can it be!

He doth give his joy to all;
He becomes an infant small;
He becomes a man of woe;
He doth feel the sorrow too.

Think not thou canst sigh a sigh
And thy maker is not by;
Think not thou canst weep a tear
And thy maker is not near.

O! he gives to us his joy
That our grief he may destroy;
Till our grief is fled and gone
He doth sit by us and moan.

WILLIAM BLAKE

SOMETIMES I feel lonely, and from the depths I cry unto Thee, and within me, Thy voice answers me, and I know that Thou, Eternal Friend, art near me.

Sometimes the sense of failure seizes me, and I am disheartened. Unto Thee I raise mine eyes, and the light of my heavenly Father shines upon me, and bids me to persevere.

Sometimes my daily life oppresses me. Unto Thee do I lift up my soul, and I realize that by doing my duty manfully and cheerfully I am serving Thee, Divine Master, and my task is revealed to me as something good and sacred.

Sometimes I am sad and sick at heart, but when I think of Thee, Spirit of perfect righteousness and love, a wonderful joy comes to me, for I know that Thou art guiding me. O Lord God of Hosts, surely Thou wilt ever comfort me. Blessed be Thy Name for ever and ever.

JUDAISM: *Fratres Book of Prayer*

O MY LORD, how certain it is that anyone who renders You some service soon pays with a great trial! And what a precious reward a trial is for those who truly love you if we could at once understand its value!

CHRISTIANITY: St. Theresa of Ávila

O THOU WHOSE tests are a healing medicine to such as are nigh unto Thee, Whose sword is the ardent desire of all those that love Thee, Whose dart is the dearest wish of those hearts that yearn after Thee, Whose decree is the sole hope of those that have recognized Thy truth! I implore Thee, by Thy divine sweetness and by the splendors of the glory of Thy face, to send down upon us from Thy retreats on high that which will enable us to draw nigh unto Thee. Set, then, our feet firm, O my God, in Thy Cause, and enlighten our hearts with the effulgence of Thy knowledge, and illumine our breasts with the brightness of Thy names.

BAHÁ'Í FAITH: Bahá'u'lláh

ABIDE WITH me; fast falls the eventide;
The darkness deepens; Lord with me abide!
When other helpers fail, and comforts flee,
Help of the helpless, O abide with me.

HENRY FRANCIS LYTE

AS A FISH that is dragged from the water gaspeth,
So gaspeth my soul.

As one who hath buried his treasure,
And now cannot find the place,
So is my mind distraught:

As a child that hath lost its mother,
So am I troubled, my heart is seared with sore anguish.

O merciful God,
Thou knowest my need,
Come, save me, and show me Thy love.

HINDUISM: *Tukaram*

I WILL LIFT up mine eyes unto the hills
    from whence cometh my help;
My help cometh from the Lord,
    which made heaven and earth.
He will not suffer thy foot to be moved:
He that keepeth thee will not slumber.
Behold, He that keepeth Israel shall neither slumber nor
    sleep.

The Lord is thy keeper:
    the Lord is thy shade upon thy right hand.
The sun shall not smite thee by day,
    nor the moon by night.
The Lord shall preserve thee from all evil:
    He shall preserve thy soul.
The Lord shall preserve thy going out and thy coming in
    from this time forth, and for evermore.

JUDAISM: *Psalm 121*

GRANT ME, dear Ahura Mazda, physical and moral strength to be Thy valiant and worthy soldier unto the end. Give me wisdom, O Wise Lord, to know and discern the truth and give me the courage to stand by truth and goodness, unfettered and undeterred by fear. Let Thy guiding hand lead me in life.

ZOROASTRIANISM

KNOW WELL, my soul, God's hand controls
    Whate'er thou fearest;
Round him in calmest music rolls
    Whate'er thou hearest.

Nothing before, nothing behind;
    The steps of faith
Fall on the seeming void, and find
    The rock beneath.

JOHN GREENLEAF WHITTIER

ALL THINGS pass
A sunrise does not last all morning
All things pass
A cloudburst does not last all day
All things pass
Nor a sunset all night
All things pass
What always changes?

Earth . . . sky . . . thunder . . .
    mountain . . . water . . .
    wind . . . fire . . . lake . . .

These change
And if these do not last

Do man's visions last?
Do man's illusions?

Take things as they come

All things pass

TAOISM: *Lao-Tzu*

FORGIVENESS AND MERCY

I HAVE SINNED against Thee, Ahura Mazda, in thought and word and deed. I have denied Thee. Intolerable is the burden of my misdoings. I have been tempted to sins and iniquities. I confess my sins to Thee, I acknowledge my sins. I humble myself before Thee. Kneeling at Thy feet, I repent. I prostrate myself before Thee to do due penance for my sins. I am fallen. Thou alone can raise me and take me by the hand.

As a penitent supplicant I come back to Thee. Forgive me for what I have done amiss. Absolve me from my sins. I approach Thee with a contrite heart, for to none else can I go but Thee.

ZOROASTRIANISM

ALMIGHTY AND most merciful Father, we have erred and strayed
from thy ways like lost sheep.
We have followed too much the devices and desires of our own
hearts.
We have offended against thy holy laws.
We have left undone those things which we ought to have
done; and we have done those things which we ought not
to have done; and there is no health in us.
But thou, O Lord, have mercy upon us, miserable offenders.
Spare thou them, O God, which confess their faults.
Restore thou them that are penitent; according to thy
promises declared unto mankind in Christ Jesu our Lord.
And grant, O most merciful Father, for his sake; that we may
hereafter live a godly, righteous, and sober life, to the
glory of thy holy Name.

CHRISTIANITY: *Book of Common Prayer*

O GOD, I seek refuge with Thee, lest I be like a servant who repented before Thee unworthily, though he had knowledge of Thy mysteries, and returned back to his transgression and his sin. Make this my penitence such that I do not need after it yet another penitence, again to put away its sequel and to abide securely.

O my God, I acknowledge my ignorance before Thee and have nought but my ill-doing wherewith to come before Thee. In Thy patience take me into the shelter of Thy mercy and hide me graciously in the curtain of Thy pardon.

O my God, I repent before Thee of all that is in the thoughts of my heart, sight of my eyes, the words of my tongue, that contravenes Thy will or falls away from Thy love . . .

O God, have mercy upon me, lonely as I am. Under Thy hand and in awe of Thee, my heart is anguished and for very fear of Thee my frame is troubled. My transgressions, O God, have brought me near to requital in the loss of Thee. Were I to keep silent none would speak for me and were I to try to intercede I have no leave or means . . .

Spread Thy mercy to take me wholly in and hide me in the Glory of Thy veil. Do with me as greatness would with a worthless servant who cried and was granted mercy or as one rich in wealth who heard a poor man's plea and refreshed him.

For, O my God, I have no defender from Thee: let Thy might be my defense and let Thy goodness be my intercessor. My sins have made me afraid: Let Thy pardon set me at rest.

ISLAM: *Ascribed to Ali, son-in-law of Muhammad*

NO DEEDS I've done nor thoughts I've thought;
Save as Thy servant, I am nought.

Guard me, O God, and O, control
The tumult of my restless soul.

Ah, do not, do not cast on me
The guilt of mine iniquity.

My countless sins, I Tuka, say,
Upon Thy loving heart I lay.

HINDUISM: *Tukaram*

GREAT SPIRIT!
Piler up of the rocks into towering mountains!
When thou stampest on the stone,
The dust rises and fills the land.
Hardness of the precipice;
Waters of the pool that turn
Into misty rain when stirred.
Vessel overflowing with oil!
Father of Runji,
Who seweth the heavens like cloth:
Let him knit together that which is below.
Caller forth of the branching trees:
Thou bringest forth the shoots
That they stand erect.
Thou hast filled the land with mankind,
The dust rises on high, oh Lord!
Wonderful One, thou livest
In the midst of the sheltering rocks,
Thou givest rain to mankind:
We pray to thee, Hear us, Lord!
Show mercy when we beseech thee, Lord.
Thou art on high with the spirits of the great.
Thou raisest the grass-covered hills
Above the earth, and createst the rivers,
Gracious One.

AFRICAN TRADITION: *Shona Hymn*

MAY THE Buddhas deign to notice me
With minds full of pity and compassion;
Established in the ten quarters of space,
May they take away my transgression.

The sin that has been done by me
Through despising mother and father,
Through not understanding the Buddhas,
And through not understanding the good;

The sin of deed, word and thought
The threefold wickedness that I have done
All that will I confess
Standing before the Buddhas.

And those that dwell in the Rose-apple land [India],
And those in other world regions
Who do good actions,
May they approve all this.

MAHAYANA BUDDHISM: *Golden Splendor Sutra*

OUR GOD and God of our fathers, let our prayer reach You – do not turn away from our pleading. For we are not so arrogant and obstinate to claim that we are indeed righteous people and have never sinned. But we know that both we and our fathers have sinned.

We have abused and betrayed. We are cruel.

We have destroyed and embittered other people's lives.

We were false to ourselves.

We have gossiped about others and hated them.

We have insulted and jeered. We have killed. We have lied.

We have misled others and neglected them.

We were obstinate. We have perverted and quarreled.

We have robbed and stolen.

We have transgressed through unkindness.

We have been both violent and weak.

We have practiced extortion.

We have yielded to wrong desires, our zeal was misplaced.

We turn away from Your commandments and good judgement but it does not help us. Your justice exists whatever happens to us, for You work for truth, but we bring about evil. What can we say before You – so distant is the place where You are found? And what can we tell You – Your being is remote as the heavens? Yet You know everything, hidden and revealed. You know the mysteries of the universe and the intimate secrets of everyone alive. You probe our body's state. You see into the heart and mind. Nothing escapes You, nothing is hidden from Your gaze. Our God and God of our fathers, have mercy on us and pardon all our sins; grant atonement for all our iniquities, forgiveness for all our transgressions.

JUDAISM

ALL THAT I ought to have thought and have not thought;
All that I ought to have said and have not said;
All that I ought to have done and have not done;
All that I ought not to have thought and yet have thought;
All that I ought not to have spoken and yet have spoken;
All that I ought not to have done and yet have done;
For thoughts, words, and works, I pray for forgiveness and
    repent with penance.

ZOROASTRIANISM: Zend-Avesta

LORD, FOR thy tender mercies' sake, lay not our sins to our charge, but forgive what is past and give us grace to amend our lives: to decline from sin and incline to virtue, that we may walk with a perfect heart before thee, now and evermore.

CHRISTIANITY: *Ridley's Prayers*

PRAISE BE unto Thee, O Lord. Forgive us our sins, have mercy upon us and enable us to return unto Thee. Suffer us not to rely on aught else besides Thee, and vouchsafe unto us, through Thy bounty, that which Thou lovest and desirest and well beseemeth Thee. Exalt the station of them that have truly believed, and forgive them with Thy gracious forgiveness. Verily, Thou art the Help in Peril, the Self-Subsisting.

BAHÁ'Í FAITH: *The Báb*

O LORD, be gracious unto us! In all that we hear or see, in all
   that we say or do, be gracious unto us.
I ask pardon of the Great God. I ask pardon at the sunset,
   when every sinner turns to Him. Now and for ever I ask
   pardon of God. O Lord, cover us from our sins, guard our
   children and protect our weaker friends.

BEDOUIN PRAYER

FOR VIOLENCE I have committed mentally,
For violence I have committed verbally,
For violence I have committed physically,
I ask forgiveness.

JAINISM

THOU DIDST ask of me love, purity and truth;
  but I was envious, sinful and untrue.
Show me mercy, Merciful!
  For if Thou refuse, no hope of deliverance have I!
Nay, my defeat I own:
  do with me according to thy own good pleasure.
Pardon if Thou wilt; or if Thou wilt,
  seize and scourge Thy erring bride.
Alas! For Thy worship I offered not my head:
  what have I done!
I have not even quaffed the nectar of Thy love,
  nor with Thy color dyed my heart;
  nor sung Thy praises with my lips;
I have achieved nothing for Thy service;
  regrets alone remain to mock my woe.
I followed in the wake of my desires,
  because I had not found my Love, my Lord:
  and O! there is no health in me.
My hope is stayed on Thee alone.
No other can my troubled soul relieve.

HINDUISM: *Dadudayal*

O MY GOD, how gentle art thou with him who has transgressed against thee: how near thou art to him who seeks thee, how tender to him who petitions thee, how kindly to him who hopes in thee.

Who is he who asked of thee and thou didst deny him, or who sought refuge in thee and thou didst betray him, or drew near to thee and thou didst hold him aloof, or fled unto thee and thou didst repulse him?

Thine, O Lord, is the creation and the authority.

By what is hidden of thy Names and by what the veils conceal of thy splendor, forgive this restless soul, this anguished heart.

O God, we seek in thee refuge from all abasement save unto thee: from all fear save thine: from all poverty save with thee.

O God, as thou hast kept our faces from prostration to any save thee, so keep our hands from being stretched out in petition to any save thee. For there is no god but thee:

Verily I was among the wrongdoers. But praise be to God, the Lord of the worlds.

SUFISM: *Naqshbandi*

A HYMN TO GOD THE FATHER

WILT THOU forgive that sin where I begun;
    Which was my sin, though it were done before?
Wilt Thou forgive that sin through which I run,
    And do run still, though still I do deplore?
When Thou hast done, Thou hast not done;
    For I have more.

Wilt Thou forgive that sin which I have won
    Others to sin, and made my sins their door?
Wilt Thou forgive that sin which I did shun
    A year or two, but wallowed in a score?
When Thou hast done, Thou hast not done;
    For I have more.

I have a sin of fear, that when I've spun
    My last thread, I shall perish on the shore;
But swear by Thyself that at my death Thy Son
    Shall shine as He shines now, and heretofore;
And having done that, Thou hast done,
    I fear no more.

JOHN DONNE

GUIDANCE

O GOD, guide me, protect me, illumine the lamp of my heart and make me a brilliant star. Thou art the Mighty and Powerful.

BAHÁ'Í FAITH: *'Abdu'l-Bahá*

BE THOU a bright flame before me,
Be thou a guiding star above me,
Be thou a smooth path below me,
Be thou a kindly shepherd behind me,
Today – tonight – and forever.

CHRISTIANITY: *St. Columba*

CLOSE MINE eyes from evil,
And my ears from hearing idle words,
And my heart from reflecting on unchaste thoughts,
And my veins from thinking of transgression.

Guide my feet to walk in thy commandments
And thy righteous ways,
And may thy mercies be turned upon me.

JUDAISM

LORD GOD ALMIGHTY,
I pray thee for thy great mercy and by the token of the holy
    rood,
Guide me to thy will, to my soul's need, better than I can
    myself;
And shield me against my foes, seen and unseen;
And teach me to do thy will that I may inwardly love thee
    before all things with a clean mind and a clean body.
For thou art my maker and my redeemer, my help, my
    comfort, my trust, and my hope.
Praise and glory be to thee now, ever and ever, world without
    end.

KING ALFRED

O HEAVENLY FATHER, in Whom we live and move and have our being, we humbly pray Thee so to guide and govern us by Thy Holy Spirit, that in all the cares and occupations of our daily life we may never forget Thee, but remember that we are ever walking in Thy sight; for Thine own Name's sake.

CHRISTIANITY: *Ancient Collect*

FROM THE unreal lead me to the real!
From darkness lead me to light!
From death lead me to immortality!

HINDUISM: *Brihad Aranyaka Upanishad*

ARISE, O Sun of Righteousness, upon us, with healing in Thy wings; make us children of the light, and of the day! Show us the way in which we should walk, for unto Thee, O Lord, do we lift up our souls. Dispel all mists of ignorance which cloud our understanding. Let no false suggestions either withdraw our hearts from the love of Thy truth, or from the practice of it in all the actions of our lives; for the sake of Jesus Christ our Lord.

CHRISTIANITY: *Bishop Sherlock*

O THOU WHOSE face is the object of my adoration, Whose beauty is my sanctuary, Whose habitation is my goal, Whose praise is my hope, Whose providence is my companion, Whose love is the cause of my being, Whose mention is my solace, Whose nearness is my desire, Whose presence is my dearest wish and highest aspiration, I entreat Thee not to withhold from me the things Thou didst ordain for the chosen ones among Thy servants. Supply me, then, with the good of this world and of the next.

Thou, truly, art the King of all men. There is no God but Thee, the Ever-Forgiving, the Most Generous.

BAHÁ'Í FAITH: *Bahá'u'lláh*

GRANT TO me, O Lord, to know what I ought to know, to love what I ought to love, to praise what delights Thee most, to value what is precious in thy sight, to hate what is offensive to Thee. Do not suffer me to judge according to the sight of my eyes, nor to pass sentence according to the hearing of the ears of ignorant men; but to discern with true judgement between things visible and spiritual, and above all things to enquire what is the good pleasure of thy will.

CHRISTIANITY: *Thomas à Kempis*

LET ME not wander in vain.
Let me not labor in vain.
Let me not mingle with the prejudiced.
Let me not leave the company of the virtuous.
Let me not fly into anger.
Let me not stray off the path of goodness.
Let me not seek for this day or for the morrow.
Give me such a wealth, O Almighty!

HINDUISM: *Pattinatar*

PROTECTION

DEAR GOD, be good to me;
The sea is so wide,
And my boat is so small.

BRETON FISHERMEN'S PRAYER

O THY Fatherly protection, O Lord, we commend ourselves and those about to travel. Bless, guide, and defend us, that we may so pass through this world as finally to enjoy in Thy Presence everlasting happiness, for Jesus Christ's sake.

SAMUEL JOHNSON

BLESSED ARE all thy Saints, O God and King, who have traveled over the tempestuous sea of this mortal life, and have made the harbor of peace and felicity. Watch over us who are still in our dangerous voyage; and remember such as lie exposed to the rough storms of trouble and temptations. Frail is our vessel, and the ocean is wide; but as in thy mercy thou hast set our course, so steer the vessel of our life toward the everlasting shore of peace, and bring us at length to the quiet haven of our heart's desire, where thou, O our God, are blessed, and livest and reignest for ever and ever.

CHRISTIANITY: *St. Augustine*

O GOD, MY God! I have set out from my home, holding fast unto the cord of Thy love, and I have committed myself wholly to Thy care and Thy protection. I entreat Thee by Thy power through which Thou didst protect Thy loved ones from the wayward and the perverse, and from every contumacious oppressor, and every wicked doer who hath strayed far from Thee, to keep me safe by Thy bounty and Thy grace. Enable me, then, to return to my home by Thy power and Thy might. Thou art, truly, the Almighty, the Help in Peril, the Self-Subsisting.

BAHÁ'Í FAITH: *Bahá'u'lláh*

O GOD, WATCH over me always, in my work, in my words, in the thoughts of my heart. O God, have mercy on me, in this world and in the world to come.

O God, have mercy on me, for I have sinned against you, mortal that I am. But kind and gentle Master, forgive me.

O God, hide not your face from me when I come before you. Do not turn away from me when you pronounce your sentence on our lives – the lives we have lived in the open and the lives that have been ours in secret.

O God, do not let me give way to disloyalty. May the enemy find nothing in me that he can call his own. O God, sharpen my will: may it be like a sword and cut out all sinful thoughts from my heart.

O God, as you calm the sea with a word, so drive out the evil passions from my sinful nature.

CHRISTIANITY: *Coptic Prayers of Dair al-Abyad*

O GOD, WHO has been the refuge of my fathers through many generations, be my refuge today in every time and circumstance of need. Be my guide through all that is dark and doubtful. Be my guard against all that threatens my spirit's welfare. Be my strength in time of testing. Gladden my heart with thy peace; through Jesus Christ my Lord.

JOHN BAILLIE

LORD, I have abandoned all for Thee,
Yet evermore desire riseth in my heart,
And maketh me forget Thy love:

Ah, save me, save me,
Save me by Thyself:

As thus I bow before Thee, Lord,
Come dwell within,
Live Thou Thy secret life in me,
And save me by Thyself.

HINDUISM: *Tukaram*

L IGHTEN OUR darkness, we beseech thee, O Lord, and by thy great mercy defend us from all perils and dangers of this night.

CHRISTIANITY: Book of Common Prayer

C AUSE US, our Father, to lie down in peace, and rise again to enjoy life. Spread over us the covering of Your peace, guide us with Your good counsel and save us for the sake of Your name. Be a shield about us, turning away every enemy, disease, violence, hunger and sorrow. Shelter us in the shadow of Your wings, for You are a God who guards and protects us, a ruler of mercy and compassion. Guard us when we go out and when we come in, to enjoy life and peace both now and forever, and spread over us the shelter of Your peace. Blessed are You Lord, who spreads the shelter of peace over us, over His people Israel, and over all the world.

JUDAISM: Daily Service

O GOD, do thou thine ear incline,
Protect my children and my kine,
E'en if thou'rt weary, still forbear,
And hearken to my constant prayer.
When shrouded 'neath the cloak of night,
Thy splendors sleep beyond our sight,
And when across the sky by day,
Thou movest, still to thee I pray.
Dread shades of our departed sires,
Ye who can make or mar desires,
Slain by no mortal hand ye dwell,
Beneath the earth, O guard us well.

AFRICAN TRADITION: *Nandi*

IN MOMENTS OF DESPAIR

GOD OF our fathers, I lie down without food,
I lie down hungry,
Although others have eaten and lie down full.
Even if it be but a polecat, or a little rock-rabbit,
Give me and I shall be grateful!
I cry to God, Father of my ancestors.

AFRICAN TRADITION: *South Africa*

BESTOW, O GOD, this grace upon us, that in the school of suffering we should learn self-conquest, and through sorrow, even if it be against our will, learn self-control.

AESCHYLUS

O GOD, THE Strength of the weak, the Comfort of the sorrowful, the Friend of the lonely: let not sorrow overwhelm Thy children, nor anguish of heart turn them from Thee. Grant that in the patience of hope and the fellowship of Christ they may continue in Thy service and in all godly living, until at length they also attain unto fullness of life before Thy face, through Jesus Christ our Lord.

CHRISTIANITY: *Methodist Book of Offices*

O MY LORD, my Beloved, my Desire! Befriend me in my loneliness and accompany me in my exile. Remove my sorrow. Cause me to be devoted to Thy beauty. Withdraw me from all else save Thee. Attract me through Thy fragrances of holiness. Cause me to be associated in Thy Kingdom with those who are severed from all else save Thee, who long to serve Thy sacred threshold and who stand to work in Thy Cause. Enable me to be one of Thy maidservants who have attained to Thy good pleasure. Verily, Thou art the Gracious, the Generous.

BAHÁ'Í FAITH: *'Abdu'l-Bahá*

SAVE ME, O God: for the waters are come in, even unto my soul.
I stick fast in the deep mire, where no ground is: I am come
  into deep waters, so that the floods run over me.
I am weary of crying; my throat is dry: my sight faileth me for
  waiting so long upon my God.

JUDAISM: Psalm 69.1–3

I HAVE no other helper than you, no other father, I pray to you.
Only you can help me. My present misery is too great.
Despair grips me, and I am at my wit's end.
O Lord, Creator, Ruler of the World, Father.
I thank you that you have brought me through.

How strong the pain was – but you were stronger.
How deep the fall was – but you were even deeper.
How dark the night was – but you were the noonday sun in it.
You are our father, our mother, our brother, and our friend.

AFRICAN TRADITION

MY BACK is broken by the conflict of my thoughts;
O Beloved One, come and stroke my head in mercy!
The palm of Thy hand on my head gives me rest,
Thy hand is a sign of Thy bounteous providence,
Remove not Thy shadow from my head,
I am afflicted, afflicted, afflicted!

SUFISM: *Rúmí*

GOD OF life, there are days when the burdens we carry chafe our shoulders and wear us down; when the road seems dreary and endless, the skies gray and threatening; when our lives have no music in them and our hearts are lonely, and our souls have lost their courage. Flood the path with light, we beseech you; turn our eyes to where the skies are full of promise.

CHRISTIANITY: *St. Augustine*

HEAR ME, O God!
    A broken heart
    Is my best part:
Use still thy rod,
That I may prove,
    Therein, Thy love.

If Thou hadst not
    Been stern to me,
    But left me free,
I had forgot
    Myself and Thee.

For, sin's so sweet,
    As minds ill-bent
    Rarely repent,
Unless they meet
    Their punishment.

Who more can crave
    Than Thou hast done?
    Thou gavest a Son
To free a slave,
    First made of nought,
    With all since bought.

Sin, death, and hell
        His glorious Name
        Quite overcame;
Yet I rebel,
        And slight the same.

But, I'll come in
        Before my loss
        Me farther toss;
As sure to win
        Under His cross.

BEN JONSON

O GOD! REFRESH and gladden my spirit. Purify my heart. Illumine my powers. I lay all my affairs in Thy hand. Thou art my Guide and my Refuge. I will no longer be sorrowful and grieved; I will be a happy and joyful being. O God! I will no longer be full of anxiety, nor will I let trouble harass me. I will not dwell on the unpleasant things of life.

O God! Thou art more friend to me than I am to myself. I dedicate myself to Thee, O Lord.

BAHÁ'Í FAITH: *'Abdu'l-Bahá*

KWAMBAZA: A CRY FOR HELP

O IMANA [GOD] of Urundi [Rwanda], if only you would help me.
O Imana of pity, Imana of my father's home [country], if only
   you would help me.
O Imana of the country of the Hutu and the Tutsi, if only you
   would help me just this once!
O Imana, if only you would give me a homestead and
   children!
I prostrate myself before you, Imana of Urundi.
I cry to you Give me offspring, give me as you give to others!
Imana, what shall I do, where shall I go?
I am in distress; where is there room for me?
O Merciful, O Imana of mercy, help me this once!

AFRICAN TRADITION: Rwanda

I BLESS THEE, Lord, for sorrows sent
    To break my dream of human power;
For now, my shallow cistern spent,
    I find thy founts, and thirst no more.

I take thy hand, and fears grow still;
    Behold thy face, and doubts remove;
Who would not yield his wavering will
    To perfect Truth and boundless Love?

That Love this restless soul doth teach
    The strength of thine eternal calm;
And tune its sad but broken speech
    To join on earth the angel's psalm.

Oh, be it patient in thy hands,
    And drawn, through each mysterious hour,
To service of thy pure commands,
    The narrow way of Love and Power.

SAMUEL JOHNSON

IN TIMES OF GRIEF

SPILL TEARS if you have grief
As tears of grief provide relief.
Strive to be straight
Try to be upright upon the Path
To fast and heave sighs of burning grief.
For the way of those acquiescent to God
Is to live with sighs and burning grief.

ISLAM: *Sha'wana*

SUPPORT US, Lord, when we are silent through grief!
Comfort us when we are bent down with sorrow! Help us
as we bear the weight of our loss! Lord, our Rock and our
Redeemer, give us strength!

JUDAISM

O LORD! THOU art the Remover of every anguish and the Dispeller of every affliction. Thou art He Who banisheth every sorrow and setteth free every slave, the Redeemer of every soul. O Lord! Grant deliverance through Thy mercy, and reckon me among such servants of Thine as have gained salvation.

BAHÁ'Í FAITH: *The Báb*

O LORD GOD, Who knowest our frame and rememberest that we are dust, look in pity upon those who mourn. Make thy loving presence so real to them that they may feel round about them thine everlasting arms, upholding and strengthening them.

Grant them such a sense of certainty that their loved one is with thee, doing thy high service, unhindered by pain, that they may turn to life's tasks with brave hearts and steady nerves, consoled in the thought that they will meet their dear one again.

Teach us all to face death unafraid and take us at last in triumph through the shadows into thine everlasting light where are reunion and never-ending joy. Through Jesus Christ our Lord.

LESLIE D. WEATHERHEAD

A BETTER RESURRECTION

I HAVE no wit, no words, no tears;
    My heart within me like a stone
Is numbed too much for hopes or fears.
    Look right, look left, I dwell alone;
I lift mine eyes, but dimmed with grief
    No everlasting hills I see;
My life is in the falling leaf:
    O Jesus quicken me.

My life is like a faded leaf,
    My harvest dwindled to a husk:
Truly my life is void and brief
    And tedious in the barren dusk;
My life is like a frozen thing,
    No bud or greenness can I see,
Yet rise it shall – the sap of Spring;
    O Jesus rise in me.

My life is like a broken bowl,
    A broken bowl that cannot hold
One drop of water for my soul
    Or cordial in the searching cold;
Cast in the fire the perished thing;
    Melt and remold it, till it be
A royal cup for Him, my King:
    O Jesus drink of me.

CHRISTINA ROSSETTI

THE LULLABY OF THE SNOW

COLD, COLD this night is my bed,
Cold, cold this night is my child,
Lasting, lasting this night thy sleep,
I in my shroud and thou in mine arm.

Over me creeps the shadow of death,
The warm pulse of my love will not stir,
The wind of the heights thy sleep-lulling,
The close-clinging snow of the peaks thy mantle.

Over thee creeps the hue of death,
White angels are floating in the air,
The Son of grace each season guards thee,
The Son of my God keeps the watch with me.

Though loud my cry, my plaint is idle,
Though sore my struggle, no friend shares it;
Thy body-shirt is the snow of the peaks,
Thy death-bed the fen of the valleys.

Thine eye is closed, thy sleep is heavy,
Thy mouth to my breast, but thou seekest no milk;
My croon of love thou shalt never know,
My plaint of love thou shalt never tell.

A cold arm-burden my love on my bosom,
A frozen arm-burden without life or breath;
May the angels of God make smooth the road,
May the angels of God be calling us home.

A hard frost no thaw shall subdue,
The frost of the grave which no spring shall make green,
A lasting sleep which morn shall not break,
The death-slumber of mother and child.

Heavenly light directs my feet,
The music of the skies gives peace to my soul,
Alone I am under the wing of the Rock,
Angels of God calling me home.

Cold, cold, cold is my child,
Cold, cold is the mother who watches thee,
Sad, sad, sad is my plaint,
As the tinge of death creeps over me.

O Cross of the heavens, sign my soul
O Mother of breastlings, shield my child,
O Son of tears whom a mother nurtured,
Show Thy tenderness in death to the needy.

CELTIC SONG

GRANT, O Lord, to all who are bereaved, the spirit of faith and courage, that they may have the strength to meet the days to come with steadfastness and patience; not sorrowing as those without hope, but in thankful remembrance of thy great goodness in past years, and in the sure expectation of a joyful reunion in the heavenly places; and this we ask in the name of Jesus Christ our Lord.

CHRISTIANITY: *Irish Prayer Book*

HEALTH AND HEALING

LAY YOUR hands gently upon us,
let your touch render your peace,
let them bring your forgiveness and healing.
Lay your hands, gently lay your hands.

You were sent to free the broken-hearted,
You were sent to give sight to the blind,
You desire to heal all our illness.
Lay your hands, gently lay your hands.

Lord, we come to you through one another.
Lord, we come to you in all our need.
Lord, we come to you seeking wholeness.
Lay your hands, gently lay your hands.

RITA J. DONOVAN

JUST AS the soft rains fill the streams,
pour into the rivers and join together in the oceans,
so may the power of every moment of your goodness
flow forth to awaken and heal all beings,
Those here now, those gone before, those yet to come.

By the power of every moment of your goodness
May your heart's wishes be soon fulfilled
as completely shining as the bright full moon,
as magically as by a wish-fulfilling gem.

By the power of every moment of your goodness
May all dangers be averted and all disease be gone.
May no obstacle come across your way.
May you enjoy fulfillment and long life.

For all in whose heart dwells respect,
who follow the wisdom and compassion, of the Way,
May your life prosper in the four blessings
of old age, beauty, happiness and strength.

BUDDHISM: *Traditional Chant (Version by Jack Kornfield)*

GUARD WELL, O Man, your share of immortality, that you may reach old age without mishap. Spirit and life I now impart to you! Do not vanish into shadow and darkness! Do not perish.

Go forth, I adjure you, into the light of the living. I draw you toward a life of a hundred autumns. Releasing you from the bonds of death and malediction, I stretch forth your life thread into the distant future.

From the Wind I have taken your breath, from the Sun your eyesight. I strengthen your heart in you, consolidate your limbs. I adjure you to speak with tongue free from stammering.

With the breath that dwells in creatures of two legs or four, I blow upon you as one blows on a fire just kindled. Let him live, not die! This man we now revive. I bring him healing. O Death, do not strike this man.

Speak in his favor! Seize him not, but release him, yours though he be. Let him stay here with all his strength! Have mercy upon him, O powers of destruction, protect him! Grant to him fullness of days, removing all evil!

Bless this man, O Death, have mercy upon him! Let him rise and depart, safe and sound, with unimpaired hearing! May he reach a hundred years and enjoy life's blessings!

We rescue him, Death, from your murky path which admits of no return, and, protecting him from the descent, we make a sheild to guard him – this is our prayer.

To you I now impart in-breath and out-breath, a ripe old age, death at its close, well-being.

HINDUISM: *Atharva Veda*

THY NAME is my healing, O my God, and remembrance of Thee is my remedy. Nearness to Thee is my hope, and love for Thee is my companion. Thy mercy to me is my healing and my succor in both this world and the world to come. Thou, verily, art the All-Bountiful, the All-Knowing, the All-Wise.

BAHÁ'Í FAITH: *Bahá'u'lláh*

HEAL US, Lord, and we shall be healed; save us, and we shall be saved; for it is You we praise. Send relief and healing for all our diseases, our sufferings and our wounds; for You are a merciful and faithful healer. Blessed are You Lord, who heals the sick.

JUDAISM: *Daily Service*

GRANT, O Lord,
to all those who are bearing pain,
thy spirit of healing,
thy spirit of life,
thy spirit of peace and hope,
of courage and endurance.
Cast out from them
the spirit of anxiety and fear;
grant them perfect confidence and trust in thee,
that in thy light they may see light,
through Jesus Christ our Lord.

ANON

BELOVED LORD, Almighty God!
Through the rays of the sun,
Through the waves of the air,
Through the All-pervading Life in space,
Purify and revivify me, and, I pray.
Heal my body, heart, and soul. Amen.

HAZRAT INAYAT KHAN

LORD, THE one that I love is sick and in great pain;
out of your compassion heal him and take away his pain.
It breaks my heart to see him suffer;
may I not share his pain if it is not your will that he be healed?
Lord, let him know that you are with him;
support and help him that he may come to know you more
deeply as a result of his suffering.
Lord be our strength and support in this time of darkness and
give us that deep peace which comes from trusting you.

ETTA GULLICK

MOTHER: O spirits of the past, this little one I hold is my child: she is your child also. Therefore, be gracious unto her.

WOMEN (*chanting*): She has come into a world of trouble: sickness is in the world, and cold and pain: the pain you knew; the sickness with which you were familiar.

MOTHER: Let her sleep in peace, for there is healing in sleep: let none among you be angry with me or with my child.

WOMEN: Let her grow; let her become strong; let her become full-grown. Then will she offer such a sacrifice to you that will delight your hearts.

AFRICAN TRADITION: *Sierra Leone*

DEATH CONSIDERS not what works be done or undone, and strikes us through our ease; a sudden thunderbolt, unsure alike for the healthy and the sick.

For the sake of things unloved and things loved have I sinned these many times, and never have I thought that I must surrender everything and depart.

Whence shall I find a kinsman, whence a friend, to protect me when the death-god's messenger seizes me? Righteousness alone can save me then, and for that I have not sought.

I come for refuge to the mighty Lords of the world [the Tathagatas], the conquerors, eager for the world's protection, who allay all fear. To the Law [Dharma] learned by them I come with all my heart for refuge, and to the congregation of the sons of enlightenment [the Bodhisattvas]. May my Lords take my transgression as it is: never more will I do this unholy work.

MAHAYANA BUDDHISM: *Santideva*

IN THE house made of dawn.
In the story made of dawn.
On the trail of dawn.
O, Talking God!
His feet, my feet, restore.
His limbs, my limbs, restore.
His body, my body, restore.
His mind, my mind, restore.
His voice, my voice, restore.
His plumes, my plumes, restore.
With beauty before him, with beauty before me.
With beauty behind him, with beauty behind me.
With beauty above him, with beauty above me.
With beauty below him, with beauty below me.
With beauty around him, with beauty around me.
With pollen beautiful in his voice, with pollen beautiful in my
    voice.
It is finished in beauty.
It is finished in beauty.
In the house of evening light.
From the story made of evening light.
On the trail of evening light.

NATIVE AMERICAN TRADITION: *Navajo*

PRAYERS AND
BLESSINGS

*Every man's life is a fairy-tale
written by God's fingers.*

HANS CHRISTIAN ANDERSEN

FOR THE YOUNG

TO THEE, the Creator, to thee, the Powerful,
I offer this fresh bud,
New fruit of the ancient tree.
Thou art the master, we thy children.
To thee, the Creator, to thee, the Powerful,
Khmvoum [God], *Khmvoum*,
I offer this new plant.

AFRICAN TRADITION: *Pygmy*

GIVE, I pray You, to all children grace reverently to love
their parents, and lovingly to obey them. Teach us all
that filial duty never ends or lessens; and bless all
parents in their children, and all children in their parents.

CHRISTINA ROSSETTI

O GOD! Rear this little babe in the bosom of Thy love and give it milk from the breast of Thy Providence. Cultivate this fresh plant in the rosegarden of Thy love and aid it to grow through the showers of Thy bounty. Make it a child of the Kingdom and lead it to Thy heavenly realm. Thou art powerful and kind, and Thou art the Bestower, the Generous, the Lord of surpassing bounty.

BAHÁ'Í FAITH: *'Abdu'l-Bahá*

FATHER WE thank Thee for the night,
And for the pleasant morning light;
For rest and food and loving care,
All that makes the day so fair.
Help us to do the things we should,
To be to others kind and good,
In all we do, in work or play,
To grow more loving every day.

ABBIE C. MORROW, *A Child's Morning Prayer*

NOW I lay me down to sleep,
I pray thee, Lord, thy child to keep;
Thy love to guard me through the night
And wake me in the morning light.

ANON: A Child's Night Prayer

I FEED YOU with the wisdom of honey. I feed you with ghee, the gift of God, the beautiful. May you have long life, protected by the Gods, may you live in this world a hundred circling years!

May God grant you intelligence, may God's power grant you intelligence, may God's two divine Messengers, lotus-wreathed, grant to you intelligence.

The Lord is full of life: through firewood God is full of life. By this vital power I make you full of life. The Divine drink is full of life. Through herbs God is full of life.

HINDUISM: Kalpa Sutras

For My Baby

O LORD, my God, shine the warm light of Your love on my
    child.
Hold her safe from all illness and harm.
Come into her little soul and comfort her with Your happiness.
Let her feel your peace.
She is too tiny to speak to me, and her cooing and gurgles are
    hard to translate into human words.
But to You, her little sounds are prayers.
Her cries are cries for Your blessing and grace.
Let her learn Your ways while she is still a child.
In adulthood, let her live the whole span of a human life,
    fulfilling Your purposes.
And in her old age, let her die joyfully, secure in the
    knowledge of Your eternal love.
I am not asking that she should be wealthy or famous, but I do
    ask that she will live prayerfully, serve others in true
    humility, loving You.
Smile on her, my God. Amen.

JOHANN STARCK

O EAGLE, O tiger, O valiant one, O my grandchild! Receive and take the water of the Lord of the World, the water which is our life, which makes the body grow and invigorates it and which serves to wash and purify. I pray that this water of celestial blue, clear blue, enter into your body and live in it. I pray that it destroy and carry away from you every ill and all the adversities that were joined in you from the beginning of the world, for we men are entrusted into her hands, she being our mother, Chalchiuhtlicue . . .

Lord, thou seest here your creature that you have sent into this place . . . Grant it, O Lord, your gifts and your breath, for thou art the great God . . .

Lady who art mother of the heavens and who is called Citlaltonac and also Citlalicue, to thee my words are directed. I implore thee to give, impress upon, and inspire this, your creature, with your power, whatever it may be . . .

O Lords, celestial gods and goddesses who dwell on high, this is your creature: Deign to implant in it your power and to blow your breath into it in order that it have life upon earth.

MEXICO: *From the Ritual Bath of the Newborn*

FATHER, O mighty force,
That force which is in everything,
Come down between us, fill us,
Until we be like thee,
Until we be like thee.

AFRICAN TRADITION: *Initiation Prayer (Guinea)*

O THOU kind Lord! These lovely children are the handiwork of the fingers of Thy might and the wondrous signs of Thy greatness. O God! Protect these children, graciously assist them to be educated and enable them to render service to the world of humanity. O God! These children are pearls, cause them to be nurtured within the shell of Thy loving-kindness.

Thou art the Bountiful, the All-Loving.

BAHÁ'Í FAITH: *'Abdu'l-Bahá*

FOR THE ELDERLY

THOU I BE OLD,
clasp me one night to thy breast,
and I,
when the dawn shall come to awaken me,
with the flush of youth on my cheek
from thy bosom
will rise.

ISLAM: *The Divan of Hafiz*

BIDE WITH us, Lord, for it is toward evening and the day is far spent; abide with us and with the whole people of God. Abide with us in the evening the day, in the evening of life, in the evening of the world. Abide with us and with all your faithful ones, O Lord, in time and eternity.

CHRISTIANITY: *Lutheran Prayer*

I INVOKE the seven daughters of Ocean
who weave the threads of the sons of age.
Three deaths be taken from me,
three life-times be given me,
seven waves of surety be granted me.
No illusions disturb my journey,
in brilliant breastplate without hurt.
My honor shall not be bound by oblivion.
Welcome age! death shall not corrupt the old.

I invoke the Silver One, undying and deathless,
may my life be enduring as white-bronze!
May my rights be upheld!
May my strength be increased!
May my grave not be dug!
May death not visit me!
May my journey be fulfilled!
I shall not be devoured by the headless adder,
nor by the hard green tick,
nor by the headless beetle.
I shall not be injured by a bevy of women
nor a gang of armed men.
May the King of the Universe stretch time for me!

CELTIC PRAYER

LORD, YOU know better than I know myself that I am growing older and will some day be old. Keep me from getting talkative, and particularly from the fatal habit of thinking that I must say something on every subject and on every occasion.

Release me from craving to straighten out everybody's affairs. Make me thoughtful but not moody; helpful but not bossy. With my vast store of wisdom it seems a pity not to use it all, but you know, Lord, that I want a few friends at the end. Keep my mind from the recital of endless details – give me wings to come to the point.

I ask for grace enough to listen to the tales of other's pains. But seal my lips on my own aches and pains – they are increasing, and my love of rehearsing them is becoming sweeter as the years go by. Help me to endure them with patience.

I dare not ask for improved memory, but for a growing humility and a lessening cocksureness when my memory seems to clash with the memories of others. Teach me the glorious lesson that occasionally it is possible that I may be mistaken.

Keep me reasonably sweet. I do not want to be a saint – some of them are so hard to live with – but a sour old woman is one of the crowning works of the devil.

Give me the ability to see good things in unexpected places, and talents in unexpected people. And give me, O Lord, the grace to tell them so.

ANON

WHEN THE signs of age begin to mark my body (and still more
    when they touch my mind); when the ill that is to
    diminish me or carry me off strikes from without or is
    born within me;
when the painful moment comes in which I suddenly waken
    to the fact that I am ill or growing old;
and above all at the last moment when I feel I am losing hold
    of myself and am absolutely passive in the hands of the
    great unknown forces that have formed me;
in all those dark moments, O God, grant that I may
    understand that it is you (provided only my faith is strong
    enough) who are painfully parting the fibers of my being
    in order to penetrate to the very marrow of my substance
    and bear me away within yourself.

PIERRE TEILHARD DE CHARDIN

OUR OLD women gods, we ask you!
Our old women gods, we ask you!
Then give us long life together,
May we live until our frosted hair
Is white; may we live till then
This life that now we know!

NATIVE AMERICAN TRADITION: *Tewa*

THOU HAST made me endless, such is thy pleasure. This frail vessel thou emptiest again and again, and fillest it ever with fresh life.

This little flute of a reed thou hast carried over hills and dales, and hast breathed through it melodies eternally new.

At the immortal touch of thy hands my little heart loses its limits in joy and gives birth to utterance ineffable.

Thy infinite gifts come to me only on these very small hands of mine. Ages pass, and still thou pourest, and still there is room to fill.

HINDUISM: *Rabindranath Tagore*

O BLESSED PAIN and sickness and fever! O welcome weariness and sleeplessness by night! Lo! God of His bounty and favor has sent me this pain and sickness in my old age; He has given me pain in the back, that I may not fail to spring up out of my sleep at midnight; that I may not sleep all night like the cattle, God in His mercy has sent me these pains. At my broken state the pity of kings has boiled up, and hell is put to silence by their threats!

Pain is a treasure, for it contains mercies; the kernel is soft when the rind is scraped off. O brother, the place of darkness and cold is the fountain of life and the cup of ecstasy. So also is endurance of pain and sickness and disease. For from abasement proceeds exaltation. The spring seasons are hidden in the autumns, and autumns are charged with springs; flee them not. Consort with grief and put up with sadness, seek long life in your own death!

SUFISM: *Rúmí*

FOR FRIENDS AND FAMILY

BLESS, O God, this dwelling,
and each who rests herein this night;
Bless, O God, my dear ones
in every place wherein they sleep;
In the night that is tonight,
and every single night;
In the day that is today,
and every single day.

CELTIC PRAYER

ALMIGHTY GOD, by whose goodness we were created, and
whose mercies never fail, we commend to thee all who
have a place in our hearts and sympathies; all who are
joined to us by the sacred ties of kindred, friendship, and love;

keep them both outwardly in their bodies and inwardly in their souls; through Jesus Christ our Lord.

JOHN HUNTER

O LORD GOD, whose will it is that, next to yourself, we should hold our parents in highest honor; it is not the least of our duties to beseech your goodness toward them. Preserve, we pray, our parents and home, in the love of your religion and in health of body, and mind. Grant that through us no sorrow may befall them; and finally as they are kind to us, so may you be to them, O supreme Father of all.

CHRISTIANITY: Desiderius Erasmus

HOLY FATHER, in your mercy,
hear our earnest prayer,
keep our loved ones, now far distant,
'neath your care.

When in sorrow, when in danger,
when in loneliness,
in your love look down and comfort
their distress.

May the joy of your salvation
be their strength and stay;
may they love and may they praise you
day by day.

ISABEL STEVENSON

GOD OF MERCY,
God of grace,
Be pleased to bless
this dwelling place.
May peace and kindly deeds
be found;
May gratitude and love
abound.

NORMA WOODBRIDGE

INTO YOUR hands, O Lord and Father, we commend our souls and bodies, our parents and our homes, friends and servants, neighbors and kindred, our benefactors and departed brethren, all your people faithfully believing and all who need your pity and protection. Enlighten us with your holy grace and suffer us never more to be separated from you, one God in Trinity, God everlasting.

EDMUND OF ABINGDON

MAY OBEDIENCE conquer disobedience with this house,
and may peace triumph over discord here,
and generous giving over avarice,
reverence over contempt,
speech with truthful words over lying utterance;
may the righteous order gain the victory
over the demon of the lie.

ZOROASTRIANISM: *Yasna*

LORD, BEHOLD our family here assembled. We thank thee for this place in which we dwell; for the love that unites us; for the peace accorded us this day; for the hope which we expect the morrow; for the health, the work, the food, and the bright skies, that make our life delightful; for our friends in all parts of the earth and our friendly helpers in this foreign isle. Let peace abound in our small community. Purge out of every heart the lurking grudge. Give us grace and strength to forbear and to persevere . . . Give us courage, gaiety and the quiet mind.

ROBERT LOUIS STEVENSON

FOR PEACE AND UNITY

LORD, MAKE me an instrument of your peace.
Where there is hatred, let me sow love;
Where there is injury, pardon;
Where there is doubt, faith;
Where there is despair, hope;
Where there is darkness, light;
Where there is sadness, joy.
O divine Master, grant that I may not so much seek
To be consoled, as to console,
To be understood, as to understand,
To be loved, as to love,
For it is in giving that we receive;
It is in pardoning that we are pardoned;
It is in dying that we are born to eternal life.

CHRISTIANITY: *St. Francis of Assisi*

LORD, WE pray for the power to be gentle; the strength to be forgiving; the patience to be understanding; and the endurance to accept the consequences of holding to what we believe to be right.

May we put our trust in the power of good to overcome evil and the power of love to overcome hatred. We pray for the vision to see and the faith to believe in a world emancipated from violence, a new world where fear shall no longer lead men to commit injustice, nor selfishness make them bring suffering to others.

Help us to devote our whole life and thought and energy to the task of making peace, praying always for the inspiration and the power to fulfill the destiny for which we and all men were created.

PRAYER FOR WORLD PEACE (1978)

GRANDFATHER,
Look at our brokenness.

We know that in all creation
Only the human family
Has strayed from the Sacred Way.

We know that we are the ones
Who are divided
And we are the ones
Who must come back together
To walk in the Sacred Way.

Grandfather,
Sacred One,
Teach us love, compassion, and honor
That we may heal the earth
And heal each other.

NATIVE AMERICAN TRADITION: *Ojibway (Canada)*

O GOD, THOU art peace. From thee is peace and unto thee is peace. Let us live, our Lord, in peace and receive us in thy paradise, the abode of peace. Thine is the majesty and the praise. We hear and we obey. Grant us thy forgiveness, Lord and unto thee be our becoming.

ISLAM: *Prayer at the Close of Salat*

O GOD, OUR Leader and our Master and our Friend, forgive our imperfections and our little motives, take us and make us one with Thy great purpose, use us and do not reject us, make us all servants of Thy kingdom, weave our lives into Thy struggle to conquer and to bring peace and union to the world.

We are small and feeble creatures, we are feeble in speech, feebler still in action; nevertheless let but Thy light shine upon us, and there is not one of us who cannot be lit by Thy fire and who cannot lose himself in Thy salvation. Take us into Thy purposes, O God; let Thy kingdom come into our hearts and into this world.

H. G. WELLS

LEAD ME from death to life,
    from falsehood to truth.
Lead me from despair to hope,
    from fear to trust.
Lead me from hate to love,
    from war to peace.
Let peace fill our heart,
    our world, our universe.
Peace. Peace. Peace.

HINDUISM: *The Upanishads*
(Adapted by Satish Kumar)

O MY GOD! O my God! Unite the hearts of Thy servants, and reveal to them Thy great purpose. May they follow Thy commandments and abide in Thy law. Help them, O God, in their endeavor, and grant them strength to serve Thee. O God! Leave them not to themselves, but guide their steps by the light of Thy knowledge, and cheer their hearts by Thy love. Verily, Thou art their Helper and their Lord.

BAHÁ'Í FAITH: *Bahá'u'lláh*

WE BESEECH thee, O Lord our God, to set the peace of heaven within the hearts of men, that it may bind the nations also in a covenant which shall not be broken, to the honor of thy holy name.

Cleanse us with the cleanness of thy truth and guide our steps in inward holiness.

Give concord and peace to us and to all living on the earth, as thou gavest to our fathers, when they prayed to thee, believing truly and ready to obey the all-powerful, the all-holy.

Grant to those who rule and lead us on earth to use aright the sovereignty thou hast bestowed upon them. Lord, make their counsels conform to what is good and pleasing unto thee, that, using with reverence and peace and gentleness the power thou hast granted them, they may find favor in thy sight. Thou only hast the means to do this, this and more than this. Glory be thine, now in the present age and age after age.

CHRISTIANITY: *St. Clement of Rome*

O HIDDEN LIFE vibrant in every atom;
O Hidden Light! shining in every creature;
O Hidden Love! embracing all in Oneness;
May each who feels himself as one with Thee,
Know he is also one with every other.

ANNIE BESANT

THE THREAT to our salvation is the clash of peoples:
Jews and Arabs,
offspring of a single father,
separated in youth by jealousy,
in adolescence by fear,
in adulthood by power,
in old age by habit.
It is time to break these habits of hate and create new habits:
habits of the heart
that will awake within us the causeless love of redemption
    and peace.

JUDAISM: *Rabbi Rami M. Shapiro*

O GOD,
Let us be united;
Let us speak in harmony;
Let our minds apprehend alike.
Common be our prayer;
Common be the end of our assembly;
Common be our resolution;
Common be our deliberations.
Alike be our feelings;
Unified be our hearts;
Common be our intentions;
Perfect be our unity.

HINDUISM: *Rig-Veda*

FOR HUMANITY

OUR GOD and God of our fathers,
Reign over the whole universe in thy glory,
And in thy splendor be exalted over all the earth.

Shine forth in the majesty of thy triumphant strength,
Over all the inhabitants of thy world,
That every form may know that thou hast formed it,
And every creature understand that thou hast created it,
And that all that hath breath in its nostrils may say:

> The Lord God of Israel is King
> And his dominion ruleth over all.

JUDAISM: *New Year Liturgy*

O GOD OUR Father, in the name of him who gave bread to the hungry, we remember all who through our human ignorance, selfishness and sin are condemned to live in want; and we pray that all endeavors for the overcoming of world poverty and hunger may be so prospered that there may be found food sufficient for all; through Jesus Christ our Lord.

CHRISTIANITY: *Christian Aid*

I FORGIVE all living beings,
Let all living beings forgive me;
All in this world are my friends,
I have no enemies.

Let the whole universe be blessed.
Let all beings be engaged in one another's well-being.
Let all weaknesses, sickness and faults be diminished and
vanish.
Let everyone, everywhere, be blissful and at peace.

JAIN SCRIPTURES

BY THE grace of God's Name
May humanity find itself lifted higher and higher.
In thy dispensation O Lord,
Let there be good in all humanity.

SIKHISM: *Guru Nanak*

WHEN YOU sit happy in your own fair house,
 Remember all poor men that are abroad,
That Christ, who gave this roof, prepare for thee
 Eternal dwelling in the house of God

ALCUIN OF YORK

I PRAY FOR the entire creation . . . for the generation which is now alive, for that which is just coming into life, and for that which shall be hereafter. And I pray for that sanctity which leads to prosperity, and which has long afforded shelter, which goes hand in hand with it, which joins it in its walk, and of itself becoming its close companion as it delivers forth its precepts, bearing every form of healing virtue which comes to us. . . . And so the greatest, and the best, and most beautiful benefits of sanctity fall like likewise to our lot.

ZOROASTRIANISM: *Zend-Avesta*

O THOU KIND Lord! Thou hast created all humanity from the same stock. Thou hast decreed that all shall belong to the same household. In Thy Holy Presence they are all Thy servants, and all mankind are sheltered beneath Thy Tabernacle; all have gathered together at Thy Table of Bounty; all are illumined through the light of Thy Providence.

O God! Thou art kind to all, Thou hast provided for all, dost shelter all, conferrest life upon all. Thou hast endowed each and all with talents and faculties, and all are submerged in the Ocean of Thy Mercy.

O Thou kind Lord! Unite all. Let the religions agree and make the nations one, so that they may see each other as one family and the whole earth as one home. May they all live together in perfect harmony.

O God! Raise aloft the banner of the oneness of mankind.

O God! Establish the Most Great Peace.

Cement Thou, O God, the hearts together.

O Thou kind Father, God! Gladden our hearts through the fragrance of Thy love. Brighten our eyes through the Light of Thy Guidance. Delight our ears with the melody of Thy Word, and shelter us all in the Stronghold of Thy Providence.

Thou art the Mighty and Powerful, Thou art the Forgiving and Thou art the One Who overlooketh the shortcomings of all mankind.

BAHÁ'Í FAITH: *'Abdu'l-Bahá*

AND NOW may God, the Soul of the Universe,
Be pleased with this my offering of words,
And being pleased may He give me
This favor in return.

That the crookedness of evil men may cease,
And that the love of goodness may grow in them.
May all beings experience from one another
The friendship of the heart.
May the darkness of sin disappear.
May the Universe see the rising of the Sun of Righteousness.
Whatever is desired, may it be received
By every living being.

May He bless the multitude of those who love God
And shower on men all forms of blessings;
May they constantly, on this earth,
Come in touch with its living beings.

May this forest of walking Wish-trees,
May this city built of living Wish-gems,
May this talking sea of nectar,
May these moons without dark spots,
May these suns without fierce heat,
May all these ever-good men,
Be the close kin of mankind.

And now in every form of happiness
May there be enjoyment to the full everywhere.
And may the Supreme Being be worshipped
For ever and ever.

HINDUISM: *Dnayaneshvari*

ETERNAL GOD, whose image lies in the hearts of all people,
We live among peoples whose ways are different from ours,
　　whose faiths are foreign to us,
　　whose tongues are unintelligible to us.
Help us to remember that you love all people with your great
　　love,
　　that all religion is an attempt to respond to you,
　　that the yearnings of other hearts are much like our own
　　and are known to you.
Help us to recognize you in the words of truth, the things of
　　beauty, the actions of love about us.
We pray through Christ, who is a stranger to no one land more
　　than another, and to every land no less than to another.

WORLD COUNCIL OF CHURCHES

LORD MOST giving and resourceful,
I implore you:
make it your will
that this people enjoy
the goods and riches you naturally give,
that naturally issue from you,
that are pleasing and savory,
that delight and comfort,
though lasting but briefly,
passing away as if in a dream.

AZTEC PRAYER

GOD OF love, whose compassion never fails; we bring to you the sufferings of all mankind; the needs of the homeless; the cry of prisoners; the pains of the sick and injured; the sorrow of the bereaved; the helplessness of the aged and weak. Strengthen and relieve them, Father, according to their various needs and your great mercy; for the sake of your Son our Savior Jesus Christ.

CHRISTIANITY: *St. Anselm*

BLESS OUR beautiful land, O Lord,
with its wonderful variety of people,
of races, cultures and languages.
May we be a nation of laughter and joy,
of justice and reconciliation,
of peace and unity,
of compassion, caring and sharing.
We pray this prayer for a true patriotism,
in the powerful name of Jesus our Lord.

CHRISTIANITY: *Archbishop Desmond Tutu*

PRAYERS FOR
SPECIAL TIMES AND
EVENTS

Prayer oneth the soul to God.

JULIAN OF NORWICH

MORNING

I REVERENTLY SPEAK in the presence of the great parent God. I pray that this day, the whole day, as a child of God, I may not be taken hold of by my own desire, but show forth the divine glory by living a life of creativeness, which shows forth the true individual.

SHINTO

F ATHER-CREATOR, Provider-from-of-old, Ancient-of-days, fresh-born from the womb of night are we. In the first dawning of the new day draw we nigh unto thee. Forlorn are the eyes till they've seen the Chief.

AFRICAN TRADITION: Bushman's Prayer
(South Africa)

THE HEAVENS are wide, exceedingly wide.
The earth is wide, very, very wide.
We have lifted it and taken it away.
We have lifted it and brought it back.
From time immemorial, the God of old bids us all abide by his
    injunctions.
Then shall we get whatever we want, be it white or red.
It is God, the Creator, the Gracious One.
Good morning to you, God, good morning.
I am learning, let me succeed.

AFRICAN TRADITION: *Akhan Drum-song*
(Ghana)

DEAR AHURA Mazda, I begin this day with Thy holy Name.
Help me to spend it usefully.

ZOROASTRIANISM

LOOK WELL to this day!
For it is life,
the very best of life.
In its brief course lie all the varieties and truths of existence;
The joy of growth,
The glory of action,
The splendor of beauty,
For yesterday is but a memory,
and tomorrow is only a vision;
But today well-lived
Makes every yesterday a memory of happiness,
And every tomorrow a vision of hope.
Look well therefore to this day!

ANCIENT SANSKRIT POEM

LET MY life be like the rainbow,
    whose colors teach us unity;
Let me follow always the great circle,
    the roundness of power,
One with the moon and the sun,
    and the ripple of waters,
Following the sacred way of honor,
    a guide and protector to the weak,
A rock of strength in my word
    that shall say no evil, no lie nor deception.
Let me be like the otter,
    so loyal to his mate he will die for her,
So strong to his children they obey him
    as the shadows obey the sun;
And let me remember always the Great One,
    the Lord of Dawning,
Whose voice whispers to me in the breeze,
    whose words come to me out of all the circles of life, and
    whose command is like the thunder:
'Be kind, be kind, be brave, be brave,
    be pure, be pure, be humble as the earth,
    and be as radiant as the sunlight!'

NATIVE AMERICAN TRADITION: *Guaymi Dawn Song*

LORD, MY joys mount as do the birds,
heavenward.
The night has taken wings
and I rejoice in the light.
What a day, Lord! What a day!

AFRICAN TRADITION: Ghana

O LORD, support us all the day long,
    until the shadows lengthen and the evening comes,
    and the busy world is hushed,
    and the fever of life is over,
    and our work is done.
Then in your mercy grant us
    a safe lodging,
    and a holy rest,
    and peace at the last.

JOHN HENRY NEWMAN

THIS DAY wilt Thou strength us. Amen
This day wilt Thou bless us. Amen
This day wilt Thou uplift us. Amen
This day wilt Thou visit us for good. Amen
This day wilt Thou inscribe us for happy life. Amen
This day wilt Thou hear our cry. Amen
This day wilt Thou accept our prayer in mercy and favor.

Amen

This day wilt Thou support us with Thy righteous hand.

Amen

JUDAISM

I HAVE WAKENED in Thy shelter, O my God, and it becometh him that seeketh that shelter to abide within the Sanctuary of Thy protection and the Stronghold of Thy defense. Illumine my inner being, O my Lord, with the splendors of the Dayspring of Thy Revelation, even as Thou didst illumine my outer being with the morning light of Thy favor.

BAHÁ'Í FAITH: *Bahá'u'lláh*

O GOD,
who hast folded back the mantle of the night
to clothe us in the golden glory of the day,
chase from our hearts all gloomy thoughts,
and make us glad with the brightness of hope,
that we may effectively aspire to unwon virtues.

CHRISTIANITY: *Ancient Collect*

AWAKE, O MAN, now is the break of day.
Thy life is running out like water from thy palm.
The bell ringeth out each hour;
the day that hath passed will not return.
The sun and moon warm thee;
thy life is drawing every day nearer to its end.
Know God within thyself.
Utter God's name alone,
and see Him in deep meditation.

HINDUISM: *Dadu*

O LORD, grant me to greet the coming day in peace.
Help me in all things to rely upon thy holy will.
In every hour of the day reveal thy will to me.
Bless my dealings with all who surround me.
Teach me to treat all that comes to me throughout the day
    with peace of soul, and with firm conviction that thy will
    governs all.
In all my deeds and words guide my thoughts and feelings.
In unforeseen events let me not forget that all are sent by
    thee.
Teach me to act firmly and wisely, without embittering or
    embarrassing others.
Give me strength to bear the fatigue of the coming day with all
    that it shall bring.
Direct my will, teach me to pray, pray thou thyself in me.

CHRISTIANITY: *Eastern Orthodox*

EVENING

M Y THANKS to Thee, dear Ahura Mazda, for a full and fruitful day.

ZOROASTRIANISM

LET SLEEP not come upon thy languid eyes
Before each daily action thou hast scanned;
What's done amiss, what done, what left undone;
From first to last examine all, and then
Blame what is wrong, in what is right rejoice.

PYTHAGORAS

IN THY name, Lord, I lay me down and in Thy name will I rise up. . . . O God, Thou art the first and before Thee there is nothing; Thou art the last and after Thee there is nothing; Thou art the outmost and above Thee there is nothing; Thou art the inmost and below Thee there is nothing. . . . Waken me, O God, in the hour most pleasing to Thee and use me in the words most pleasing to Thee, that Thou mayest bring me ever nearer to Thyself.

ISLAM: *Al-Ghazzálí*

O LORD MY God, thank you for bringing this day to a close;
Thank you for giving me rest in body and soul.
Your hand has been over me and has guarded and preserved
    me.
Forgive my lack of faith and any wrong that I have done today,
    and help me to forgive all who have wronged us.
Let me sleep in peace under your protection, and keep me
    from all the temptations of darkness.
Into your hands I commend my loved ones and all who dwell
    in this house;
I commend to you my body and soul.
    O God, your holy name be praised.

DIETRICH BONHOEFFER

BLESSED ART Thou, O Lord our God, King of the universe,
Who makest the bands of sleep to fall upon mine eyes,
And slumber upon mine eyelids.

May it be Thy will, O Lord my God and God of my fathers,
To suffer me to lie down in peace
And to let me rise up again in peace.

Let not my thoughts trouble me,
Nor evil dreams, nor evil fancies,
But let my rest be perfect before Thee.

O lighten mine eyes, lest I sleep the sleep of death,
For it is Thou who givest light to the apple of the eye.
Blessed art Thou, O Lord,
Who givest light to the whole world in Thy glory.

JUDAISM

O GOD, YOU have let me pass this day in peace,
let me pass the night in peace.
O Lord who has no Lord,
there is no strength but in Thee.
Thou alone hast no obligation.
Under Thy hand I pass the night.
Thou art my mother and my father.

AFRICAN TRADITION: *Boran (Kenya)*

WATCH, DEAR Lord, with those who wake, or watch, or weep
    tonight, and give your angels charge over those who sleep.
Tend your sick ones, O Lord Christ,
rest your weary ones,
bless your dying ones,
soothe your suffering ones,
pity your afflicted ones,
shield your joyous ones.
And all for your love's sake.

CHRISTIANITY: *St. Augustine*

SO FAVOR us this night,
>O Thou whose pathways we have visited
>as birds who nest upon a tree.
Night hath put all her glories on;
>the villagers who sought their homes,
>and all that walks and all that flies.
Keep wolf and thief away;
>from falling lightnings keep us safe
>great King of all the mighty world.

HINDUISM: *Rig-Veda*

IN THE night of weariness let me give myself up to sleep
without struggle, resting my trust upon Thee.
Let me not force my flagging spirit into a poor preparation for
Thy worship.
It is Thou who drawest the veil of night upon the tired eyes of
the day to renew its sight in a fresher gladness of
awakening.

SIKHISM: *Sadhu Sundar Singh*

NOW THAT evening has fallen,
To God, the Creator, I will turn in prayer,
Knowing that he will help me.
I know the Father will help me.

AFRICAN TRADITION: Dinka (Sudan)

ABIDE WITH us, O most blessed and merciful Savior, for it is toward evening and the day is far spent. As long as Thou art present with us, we are in the light. When Thou art present all is brightness, all is sweetness. We discourse with Thee, watch with Thee, live with Thee and lie down with Thee. Abide then with us, O Thou whom our soul loveth; Thou Sun of righteousness with healing under Thy wings arise in our hearts; make Thy light then, to shine in darkness as a perfect day in the dead of night.

HENRY VAUGHAN

HOW CAN I choose to sleep, O God, my God, when the eyes of them that long for Thee are wakeful because of their separation from Thee; and how can I lie down to rest whilst the souls of Thy lovers are sore vexed in their remoteness from Thy presence?

I have committed, O my Lord, my spirit and my entire being into the right hand of Thy might and Thy protection, and I lay my head on my pillow through Thy power, and lift up according to Thy will and Thy good pleasure. Thou art, in truth, the Preserver, the Keeper, the Almighty, the Most Powerful.

By Thy might! I ask not, whether sleeping or waking, but that which Thou dost desire. I am Thy servant and in Thy hands. Graciously aid me to do what will shed forth the fragrance of Thy good pleasure. This, truly, is my hope and the hope of them that enjoy near access to Thee. Praised be Thou, O Lord of the worlds!

BAHÁ'Í FAITH: *Bahá'u'lláh*

WE WAIT in the darkness!
Come, all ye who listen,
Help in our night journey.
Now no sun is shining;
Now no star is glowing;
Come show us the pathway;
The night is not friendly;
The moon has forgot us.
We wait in the darkness!

NATIVE AMERICAN TRADITION: *Iroquois*

I REVERENTLY SPEAK in the presence of the great parent God. I give Thee grateful thanks that Thou hast enabled me to live this day, the whole day, in obedience to the excellent spirit of Thy ways.

SHINTO

BIRTH

MY LORD! My Lord! I praise Thee and I thank Thee for that whereby Thou hast favored Thine humble maid-servant, Thy slave beseeching and supplicating Thee, because Thou hast verily guided her unto Thine obvious Kingdom and caused her to hear Thine exalted Call in the contingent world and to behold Thy Signs which prove the appearance of Thy victorious reign over all things.

O my Lord, I dedicate that which is in my womb unto Thee. Then cause it to be a praiseworthy child in Thy Kingdom and a fortunate one by Thy favor and Thy generosity; to develop and to grow up under the charge of Thine education. Verily, Thou art the Gracious! Verily, Thou art the Lord of Great Favor!

BAHÁ'Í FAITH: *'Abdu'l-Bahá*

I CUT THE cord
Those scissors in hand
We are no longer
the same

Praise a Lord!
Un hijo, a Son, a Boy!
Two more feet touch the earth!

JOE RICHEY

A HUSBAND'S AND FATHER'S PRAYER

ALL ASSEMBLED: O fathers and ancestors, and all who are of the near and far past, bear witness: we cry to thee (God) to let this child be safely born.

HUSBAND: If I have sinned, be merciful, and if thou canst not be merciful, then punish me, slay me: but heal this woman and let this child live.

FATHER (of the woman): This is my daughter: she is in your hands: spare her life, and give her a living child.

AFRICAN TRADITION: Sierra Leone

THAT SHE was taken out of her mother,
thanks be for that!
That she, the little one,
was taken out of her, we say,
thanks be for that!

WEST GREENLAND ESKIMO SONG

GIVE HEED, my child, lift your eyes,
behold the one who is standing here.
Behold, my child! Waiting now to fit
and set you here apart.
Give heed, my child. Look!
Sacred ointment now is here come to you.

Give heed, my child, lift your eyes,
behold the one who has holy made.
Behold, my child! You are set apart,
and finished is the task.
Give heed, my child. Look!
Sacred ointment now has set you apart.

NATIVE AMERICAN TRADITION: Pawnee Song

NEWBORN, ON the naked sand
Nakedly lay it
Next to the earth mother,
That it may know her;
Having good thoughts of her, the food giver.

Newborn, we tenderly
In our arms take it,
Making good thoughts.

House-god, be entreated,
That it may grow from childhood to manhood,
Happy, contented;
Beautifully walking
The trail to old age.
Having good thoughts of the earth its mother,
That she may give it the fruits of her being.

Newborn, on the naked sand
Nakedly lay it.

NATIVE AMERICAN TRADITION: *Pueblo*

MARRIAGE

WE SWEAR by peace and love to stand
Heart to heart and hand in hand.
Mark, O Spirit, and hear us now,
Confirming this our Sacred Vow.

DRUIDIC VOW

I ADD MY breath to your breath
that our days may be long on the Earth,
that the days of our people may be long,
that we shall be as one person,
that we may finish our road together.

NATIVE AMERICAN TRADITION: *Pueblo*

THE TWAIN in one are joined today. May their right hands be tied by the bond of love in lasting union. May the mind of one blend with the mind of the other and the heart be in tune with the heart. May the twin spirits be one spirit in joy and sorrow, success and failure, prosperity and adversity. May the two come nearer to each other in good thoughts, good words, and good deeds from day unto day.

May each transmit something good to the other. May each take the best that is in the other, and give something better than the best. May each give in goodness what the other lacks and may they give mutual completion to each other in life.

Locked in the embrace of wedded love, may they live for each other, may they share each other's feelings, may they lighten each other's load in life, and may they live in the loving fellowship of minds and hearts. May each elevate and embellish what nature has bestowed on the other. With hearts knitted together, may the two be the whole world to each other. May each one be life for the other. May he be hers and she be his wholly for all the days of their lives. May each cleave faithfully unto each in body and mind and spirit as the vine that twines its tendrils around the tall tree. May better than the best come unto them. May it be so even as we pray, *Ahura Mazda*. Amen.

ZOROASTRIANISM: *Wedding Ceremony*

GLORY BE unto Thee, O my God! Verily, this Thy servant and this Thy maidservant have gathered under the shadow of Thy mercy and they are united through Thy favor and generosity. O Lord! Assist them in this Thy world and Thy kingdom and destine for them every good through Thy bounty and grace. O Lord! Confirm them in Thy servitude and assist them in Thy service. Suffer them to become the signs of Thy Name in Thy world and protect them through Thy bestowals which are inexhaustible in this world and the world to come. O Lord! They are supplicating the kingdom of Thy mercifulness and invoking the realm of Thy singleness. Verily, they are married in obedience to Thy command. Cause them to become the signs of harmony and unity until the end of time.

Verily, Thou art the Omnipotent, the Omnipresent and the Almighty!

BAHÁ'Í FAITH: *'Abdu'l-Bahá*

UNITED YOUR resolve, united your hearts,
may your spirits be at one,
that you may long together dwell
in unity and concord.

HINDUISM: Rig-Veda

THAT I may come near to her, draw me nearer to Thee than to her; that I may know her, make me to know Thee more than her; that I may love her with the perfect love of a perfectly whole heart, cause me to love Thee more than her and most of all. Amen. Amen.

That nothing may be between me and her, be Thou between us, every moment. That we may be constantly together, draw us into separate loneliness with Thyself. And when we meet breast to breast, my God, let it be on Thine own. Amen. Amen.

TEMPLE GAIRDNER

MAY THE Great Spirit send his choicest gifts to you.
May the Sun father and Moon mother
shed their softest beams on you.
May the four winds of heaven glow gently upon you
and upon those with whom you share your heart and home.

MEXICO: *Coahuila Blessing*

ENTREAT ME not to leave thee,
　　Or to return from following after thee:
For wither thou goest, I will go,
　　And where thou lodgest, I will lodge.
Thy people shall be my people,
　　And thy God my God.
Where thou diest, will I die,
　　And there will I be buried.
The Lord do so to me, and more also,
　　If ought but death part me from thee.

JUDAISM: *Ruth 1.16–17*

WE PRAY, dear Ahura Mazda, with our hearts full of gratitude, that you bless us, help us and guide us as we start our lives together, and always be with us and with all those whom we love and cherish.

ZOROASTRIANISM

MAY THESE vows and this marriage be blessed.
May it be sweet milk,
    this marriage, like wine and halvah.
May this marriage offer fruit and shade
    like the date palm.
May this marriage be full of laughter,
    our every day a day in paradise.
May this marriage be a sign of compassion,
    a seal of happiness here and hereafter.
May this marriage have a fair face and a good name,
    an omen as welcome as the moon in a clear blue sky.
I am out of words to describe
    how spirit mingles in this marriage.

SUFISM: Rúmí

DEATH AND THE LIFE BEYOND

ANTICIPATING ONE'S OWN DEATH

MY LORD, it is time to move on.
Well, then, may Your will be done.
O my Lord and my Spouse,
the hour that I have longed for has come.
It is time for us to meet one another.

CHRISTIANITY: *St. Theresa of Ávila*

DEATH IS a bridge between friends. The time now nears
that I cross that bridge, and friend meets Friend.

ISLAM: *Rábi'a*

CROSSING THE BAR

SUNSET AND evening star
 And one clear call for me!
And may there be no moaning of the bar
 When I put out to sea,

But such a tide as moving seems asleep,
 Too full for sound and foam,
When that which drew from out the boundless deep
 Turns again home.

Twilight and evening bell,
 And after that the dark!
And may there be no sadness of farewell,
 When I embark;

For tho' from our borne of Time and Place
 The flood may bear me far,
I hope to see my Pilot face to face
 When I have crossed the bar.

ALFRED, LORD TENNYSON

IN THE rising of the sun and in its going down,
   we remember them.
In the glowing of the wind and in the chill of winter,
   we remember them.
In the opening of buds and in the rebirth of spring,
   we remember them.
In the blueness of the sky and in the warmth of summer,
   we remember them.
In the rustling of leaves and in the beauty of autumn,
   we remember them.
In the beginning of the year and when it ends,
   we remember them.
When we are weary and in need of strength,
   we remember them.
When we are lost and sick at heart,
   we remember them.
When we have joys we yearn to share,
   we remember them.
So long as we live, they too shall live,
   for they are now a part of us, as
   we remember them.

JUDAISM

Death and the Life Beyond ⁓ 195

LORD, I am coming as far as I can. I know I must pass through the shadow of death, before I can come to Thee. But it is but a mere shadow, a little darkness upon nature: but Thou, by Thy merits and passion, hast broken through the jaws of death. So, Lord, receive my soul, and have mercy upon me.

WILLIAM LAUD, *spoken before his execution*

THE TRAVELER has reached the end of the journey! In the freedom of the Infinite he is free from all sorrows: the fetters that bound him are thrown away, and the burning fever of life is no more.

BUDDHISM: *Dhammapada*

DEATH HAS freed . . . from his material bondage. He has shed his frail earthly mansion and departed this life to live hereafter in the realm of the spirit. His earthly work is done and he has laid down his burden. From the din and dust of life's struggle, he has gone to the deathless world of peace and rest where light fades not and happiness fails not. Our beloved has died in body to live in spirit a life higher and nobler than our thoughts can measure and minds can conceive. Let him rest in everlasting peace and joy with Thee, Ahura Mazda.

ZOROASTRIANISM: *Funeral Prayer*

VITAL SPARK of heavenly flame!
Quit, O quit this mortal frame!
Trembling, hoping, lingering, flying,
O the pain, the bliss of dying!
Cease, fond Nature, cease thy strife,
And let me languish into life!

Hark! they whisper; angels say,
'Sister spirit, come away!'
What is this absorbs me quite?
Steals my senses, shuts my sight,
Drowns my spirits, draws my breath?
Tell me, my soul, can this be death?

The world recedes; it disappears!
Heaven opens on my eyes, my ears
With sounds seraphic ring.
Lend, lend your wings! I mount! I fly!
O Grave! where is thy victory?
O Death! where is thy sting!

ALEXANDER POPE

IN THE great night my heart will go out;
Toward me the darkness comes rustling.
In the great night my heart will go out.

PAPAGO PRAYER

O LORD, MAY the end of my life be the best of it; may my closing acts be my best acts, and may the best of my days be the day when I shall meet Thee.

ISLAM

O GOD, WHEN we try to obliterate the frontier of clouds which separates us from the other world, guide our unpracticed movements. And, when the given hour shall strike, arouse us, eager as the traveller who straps on his rucksack while beyond the misty window-pane earliest rays of dawn are faintly visible.

GABRIEL MARCEL

GOING TO Heaven!
I don't know when –
Pray do not ask me how!
Indeed I'm too astonished
To think of answering you!
Going to Heaven!
How dim it sounds!
And yet it will be done
As sure as flocks go home at night
Unto the Shepherd's arm!

Perhaps you're going too!
Who knows?
If you should get there first
Save just a little space for me
Close to the two I lost –
The smallest 'Robe' will fit me
And just a bit of 'Crown' –
For you know we do not mind our dress
When we are going home –

EMILY DICKINSON

Death and the Life Beyond 199

GRIEF ON ANOTHER'S DEATH

FAREWELL, my younger brother.
From the highest places
The Gods have come for me.
You will never see me again.
But when the showers pass over you,
And the thunder sounds,
You will pray:
"There is the voice of my elder brother."
And when the harvests ripen,
And you hear the voices
of all the small beautiful birds,
And the grasshoppers chirp,
You will pray:
"There is the voice of my elder brother;
There is the trail of his soul."

NATIVE AMERICAN TRADITION: *Navajo*

WITH SILENCE only as their benediction
    God's angels come,
Where, in the shadow of a great affliction,
    The soul sits dumb.

Yet would we say, what every heart approveth,
    Our Father's will,
Calling to him the dear ones whom he loveth,
    Is mercy still.

Not upon us or ours the solemn angel
    Hath evil wrought;
The funeral anthem is a glad evangel –
    The good die not!

God calls our loved ones, but we love not wholly
    What he has given;
They live on earth in thought and deed as truly
    As in his heaven.

JOHN GREENLEAF WHITTIER

O MY GOD! O Thou forgiver of sins, bestower of gifts, dispeller of afflictions!

Verily, I beseech Thee to forgive the sins of such as have abandoned the physical garment and have ascended to the spiritual world.

O my Lord! Purify them from trespasses, dispel their sorrows, and change their darkness into light. Cause them to enter the garden of happiness, cleanse them with the most pure water, and grant them to behold Thy splendors on the loftiest mount.

BAHÁ'Í FAITH: *'Abdu'l-Bahá*

THOU GOEST home this night to thy home of winter,
To thy home of autumn, of spring, and of summer;
Thou goest home this night to thy perpetual home,
To thine eternal bed, to thine eternal slumber.

Sleep thou, sleep, and away with thy sorrow;
Sleep thou, sleep, and away with thy sorrow;
Sleep thou, sleep, and away with thy sorrow;
Sleep thou, beloved, in the Rock of the fold . . .

The shade of death lies upon thy face, beloved,
But the Jesus of grace has His hand round about thee;
In nearness to the Trinity farewell to thy pains,
Christ stands before thee and peace is in His mind.

Sleep, O sleep in the calm of all calm,
Sleep, O sleep in the guidance of guidance,
Sleep, O sleep in the love of all loves,
Sleep, O beloved, in the Lord of life,
Sleep, O beloved, in the God of life!

CELTIC PRAYER

O GREAT NZAMBI, what thou hast made is good, but thou hast brought a great sorrow to us with death. Thou shouldst have planned in some way that we would not be subject to death. O Nzambi, we are afflicted with great sadness.

AFRICAN TRADITION: Funeral Chant (Congo)

WE GIVE back, to you, O God, those whom you gave to us. You did not lose them when you gave them to us, and we do not lose them by their return to you. Your dear Son has taught us that life is eternal and love cannot die. So death is only an horizon, and an horizon is only the limit of our sight. Open our eyes to see more clearly, and draw us closer to you that we may know that we are nearer to our loved ones, who are with you. You have told us that you are preparing a place for us; prepare us also for that happy place, that where you are we may also be always, O dear Lord of life and death.

WILLIAM PENN

ACKNOWLEDGEMENTS

Every effort has been made to trace and acknowledge ownership of copyright. If any required credits have been omitted or any rights overlooked, it is completely unintentional. The publishers will be glad to make suitable arrangements with any copyright holder whom it has not been possible to contact, and would like to acknowledge the following for permission to reproduce material in this book.

Annie Besant, "O Hidden Life vibrant in every atom . . " reprinted with kind permission of the Theosophical Society in England • D. Bonhoeffer, selection from *Letters and Papers from Prison, the Enlarged Edition*, SCM Press, 1971 • "i thank You God for most this amazing," © 1950 © 1978, 1991 the Trustees for the e.e. Cummings Trust © 1979 by George James Firmage, from *Complete Poems: 1904–1962* by e.e. Cummings, Edited by George J. Firmage. Reprinted by permission of Liveright Publishing Corporation • Chandra Devanesen from *Morning, Noon and Night* edited by Rev. John Carden. Used by permission of the Church Mission Society • Selection by Rita J. Donovan excerpted from *Prayers for Healing* © Maggie Oman. Reprinted by permission of Conari Press • "Lord, the one that I love..." © Etta Gullick • Selection by Charles Kingsley reproduced by permission of Mrs A.M.K. Covey-Crump • The Society of Authors is the literary representative of the Estate Katherine Mansfield • Reinhold Niebuhr from "The Serenity Prayer", by permission of Harper Collins • Selection by Christina Rossetti by permission of Louisiana State University Press • Rabbi Rami M. Shapiro. "Clash" from *Lived Knowing: Psalms and Other Poems* by Rabbi Rami M. Shapiro. Reprinted by permission of the author • Rabindranath Tagore: from "Gitanjali", in *Collected Poems and Plays* © 1916 by Macmillan Publishing Co., Inc., renewed 1944 by Rabindranath Tagore. Used by permission of Macmillan, London and Basingstoke, and Macmillan Publishing Co., Inc. • Teilhard de Chardin: from *Le Milieu Divin* • "Bless our beautiful land, O Lord" spoken by Archbishop Desmond Tutu at the inauguration of Nelson Mandela as State President of South Africa in Pretoria in 1994 • Evelyn Underhill: from *Meditations and Prayers* (privately printed)• L. Weatherhead, *A Private House of Prayer*, Arthur James Ltd. • Norma Woodbridge. "Prayers for Our Home" from *Graces* by June Cotner. Reprinted by permission of the author

INDEX OF AUTHORS AND SOURCES